GOD AND FAITH OF THE FAITHFUL

SIMPLIFYING THE CATHOLIC FAITH FOR THE LAITY

BOSCO EKKA | SDB

Contents

Preface

The intention of this book is to develop a correct way of understanding the catholic faith for the laity that can be of help and value in the mission of the Church, especially, in the context of the new evangelization. The writer thinks a book is needed to help the young laity grow to be a better human person in the church and in the society at large. In this way as a Salesian, the writer also wanted to assist our young laity to discover and appreciate their roles in the church and in the society.

To serve the pastoral purposes of the book, the writer in chapter one introduces the book with the "Word of God". The following chapters discuss the **Reign of God** in the Father's plan of Creation, in the historical ministry of Jesus, in the permanent action of the Holy Spirit, in the liturgy and in the mission of the Church; the **Trinitarian life of God** (mystery-communion-mission) as revealed by Jesus Christ; the Church as "icon" of the Trinity and universal sacrament of salvation; and every baptized as a sharer in the Trinitarian life of God; **the Paschal Mystery of Jesus:** a historically documented event, a mystery of faith, the core of life and Christian proclamation; **Divine Filiation** "God became man so that man could become God." In Jesus Christ, we are "children of God" – the Trinitarian, liturgical-sacramental, moral and ecclesiological dimension of our divine filiation; **The Church** as the "living" work of the Holy Spirit; unity, holiness, catholicity and apostolicity as dynamic endowments of the Holy Spirit to the Church, as well as task that challenge the Church as she continues Christ's mission on earth; **The Eucharist** as "memorial", "mystery of faith", "paschal sacrifice", "eschatological summit", grace and summit of the life of the ecclesial community; **Christian Life** as life in Christ directed to God: faith-hope-charity as grace of connaturality and as personal response in communion with God and with others; The Fundamental principles of Christian Action(Work): "to imitate the Father" (c.f. Mt 5:48; Lk 6:36), "to live Christ" (cf. Rom 8:1), "to walk in the Spirit" (cf.Gal.5:25) are all based on the dynamics between freedom, conscience, grace, sin, and virtues in a person; From Christ, "servant" of the Father, to the Church, servant of Christ, to the Christian, servant of humankind: the reality and concept of **DIAKONIA** in the Bible and Theological Reflection; and the final chapter talks about the **Liturgy** (Mystery-celebration-life) is the exercise of the priesthood of Christ which all the members of the Church take part as consecrated by the Holy Spirit for the glory of the Father and for the sanctification of humankind.

The writer made use of three domains:(*Christology, Pneumatology, Ecclesiology, Moral Theology, Liturgy, Spiritual Theology)* as the overall methods in the book. The writer, along with his congregation, hopes that through this book, he has achieved his purpose of studies in the Don Bosco Center of Studies. Although, with his own limitations, he acknowledges the need for constant updating and enhancement of both himself and the book he designed.

Acknowledgements

First and foremost, I would like to thank God for the light of His inspiration which has sustained me in the course of finishing this project paper. It was only through His grace and love that this entire intellectual pursuit was made possible.

To Rev. Fr. Henry Mark Bonetti, SDB, my book adviser, I appreciate all the assistance you have provided for me from the planning to the development stage of this study. Thank you for your patience, kindness and advice which made me value even more the great teaching that is Salesian.

To Br. Ferrer Joe, SDB, for your loving kindness and patience to guide and suggesting and correcting the English of my project paper. Thank you, brother.

To the Don Bosco Center of Studies and to all my professors, thank you for showing me that there is unspeakable joy in studying about God and true completion in serving the Lord.

To my Salesian Brothers and Priests in those communities that I have been to, thank you for your support and good example, especially for to journey with you in this finishing this project paper. Your love and commitment to God have been always a source of great inspiration. To the young people, I am blessed to have met and would meet each one of you in my life in the mission that I am sent. Thank you.

Finally, to St. John Bosco and Salesians Saints, thank you for the inspiration and intercession in finishing this book. I am forever grateful for everything you have taught us and offer your life for the sake of your people. You have inspired me to see myself through the Father's eyes.

CHAPTER ONE

The Word of God

Divine Revelation

"In his goodness and wisdom God chose to reveal Himself and to make known to us the hidden purpose of his Will…"[1] The divine plan of God is "through Christ, the Word made flesh, a man might in the Holy Spirit have access to the Father and come to share in the divine nature."[2] In order word, God wants us to be his adopted sons and daughters through Jesus Christ and the Holy Spirit so that we are able to share with Him his eternal life and happiness.

In order to communicate his loving plan to man, God uses divine revelation. Through divine revelation, God speaks to man as friends. This makes our religion unique and the highest rank religion. Only in Christianity, can we find the God who speaks to his people. "Through divine revelation, God chose to show forth and communicate Himself and the eternal decisions of His will regarding the salvation of men."[3] He wants all men to know his loving plan with ease and absolute certainty in order to be saved and become his sons and daughters.

God reveals Himself through deeds and words. "The deeds wrought by God in the history of salvation manifest and confirm the teaching and realities signified by the words, while the words proclaim the deeds and clarify the mystery contained in them."[4]

The handing on of Divine Revelation

Divine Revelation is handed on through Sacred Tradition and Sacred Scripture. "Sacred tradition and Sacred Scripture form one deposit of the word of God."[5] They are interrelated. We cannot separate them because they have the same origin: God.

Only the Catholic Church has the authority to interpret Divine Revelation. "The task of authentically interpreting the word of God, whether written or handed on, has been entrusted exclusively to the living teaching office of the Church, whose authority exercised in the name of Jesus Christ."[6] The Church has the responsibility to preserve, guard and proclaim it authentically to the people of God.

"Sacred Tradition, Sacred Scripture and the teaching authority of the Church, in accord with God's most wise design, are so linked and joined together that one cannot stand without the others." Those three all "altogether and each in its own way under the action of the one Holy Spirit contribute effectively to the salvation of souls."[7]

The Old Testament

The Old Testament is a collection of 46 books belonging to three categories: historical, prophetic and wisdom books.

We can find in the Old Testament the plan of salvation written and explained by the sacred authors. These books are written under divine inspiration and "remain permanently valuable."[8]

The purpose of the Old Testament is to prepare for the coming of Christ. It reveals to all men "the knowledge of God and of man and the ways in which God, just and merciful, deals with men."[9] Those books in the Old Testament also contain "a store of sublime teachings about God, sound wisdom about human life, and a wonderful treasury of prayers, and in them, the mystery of our salvation is present in a hidden way."[10]

The New Testament

The New Testament contains the four Gospels, the epistles of Saint Paul and other apostolic writings. They were composed under the inspiration of the Holy Spirit. Among those writings, the Gospels have a special place because "they are the principal witness for the life and teaching of the incarnate Word, our saviour."[11]

There is a close relationship between the Old and the New Testament. "God, the inspirer and author of both Testaments, wisely arranged that the New Testament be hidden in the Old and the Old be made manifest in the New."[12]

The focus of the New Testament is Jesus Christ. As described, "When the fullness of time arrived, the Word was made flesh and dwelt among us in His fullness of graces and truth. Christ established the Kingdom of God on earth, manifested His Father and Himself by deeds and words, and completed his work by His death, resurrection and glorious Ascension and by the sending of the Holy Spirit. Having been lifted up from the earth, He draws all men to Himself, He who alone has the words of eternal life."[13] The rest of the New Testament is about the development of the early Church.

The Word of God in the Church

The word of God has a vital role in the life of the Church. "For in the Sacred Books, the Father who is in heaven meets His children with great love and speaks with them, and the force and power in the word of God is so great that it stands as the support and energy of the Church, the strength of faith for her sons, the food for the soul, the pure and everlasting source of spiritual life."[14]

Therefore, "The easy access to Sacred Scripture should be provided for all the Christian faithful...The Church by her authority with maternal concern sees to it that suitable and correct translations are made into different languages, especially from the original texts of the sacred books."[15]

"The Christian life is essentially marked by an encounter with Jesus Christ, who calls us to follow him."[16] Knowledge of the Sacred Scriptures is an indispensable means to know, love and follow Christ. Therefore, the Church always strives to understand the word of God deeper. She encourages everybody especially the theologians to "devote their energies, under the watchful care of the sacred teaching office of the Church, to an exploration and exposition of the divine writings."[17] Here we find the place of theology. "Sacred theology rests on the written word of God, together with sacred tradition, as its primary and perpetual foundation."[18] Therefore, studying Sacred scripture is the soul of sacred theology.

The word of God is proclaimed mostly through pastoral preaching, catechetics, all Christian instruction and especially through the liturgical homilies. Therefore, those who are involved directly in this ministry of the Word especially the priests of Christ, deacons and catechists "must hold fast to the Sacred Scriptures through diligent sacred reading and careful study."[19]

The Proclamation of the Word of God

Jesus Christ himself commissioned to the Apostles the very noble task of bringing Good News to his people. "And he said to them, 'Thus it is written that the Messiah would suffer and rise from the dead on the third day and that repentance, for the forgiveness of sins, would be preached in his name to all the nations, beginning from Jerusalem'." (Luke 24:46) Because of that, all the members of the Church, all bishops, priests, religious, laymen and women are called to this mission.

"The Church is missionary by her very nature. We cannot keep to ourselves the words of eternal life given to us in our encounter with Jesus Christ: they are meant for everyone, for every man and woman."[20] "The Church's mission cannot be considered as an optional or supplementary element in her life. Rather it entails letting the Holy Spirit assimilate us to Christ himself, and this to share in his own mission: 'As the Father has sent me, so I send you (John 20:21) to share the word with your entire life."[21]

Witness of the baptized is an important part in proclaiming the word of God. "It is important that every form of proclamation keep in mind, first of all, the intrinsic relationship between the communication of God's word and Christian witness."[22]

It is necessary that the proclamation of the word of God entails the tireless effort to foster justice, peace and to lift up the cultures and environments of the societies.

[1] Vatican II, Dei Verbum, no 2
[2] Ibid, no 2
[3] Ibid, no 6
[4] Ibid, no 2

[5] Vatican II, Dei Verbum, no 10

[6] Vatican II, Dei Verbum, no 10

[7] Vatican II, Dei Verbum, no 10

[8] Vatican II, Dei Verbum, no 14

[9] Vatican II, Dei Verbum, no 15

[10] Vatican II, Dei Verbum, no 15

[11] Vatican II, Dei Verbum, no 18

[12] Vatican II, Dei Verbum, no 16

[13] Vatican II, Dei Verbum, no 17

[14] Vatican II, Dei Verbum, no 21

[15] Vatican II, Dei Verbum, no 22

[16] Pope Benedict XVI, Verbum Domini, no 72

[17] Vatican II, Dei Verbum, no23

[18] Vatican II, Dei Verbum, no24

[19] Vatican II, Dei Verbum, no25

[20] Pope Benedict XVI, Verbum Domini, no 91

[21] Pope Benedict XVI, Verbum Domini, no 93

[22] Pope Benedict XVI, Verbum Domini, no 97

CHAPTER TWO

Transmission of Revelation:- Word

Revelation- comes from the Latin word revelare which means to remove the veil.

God reveal to man

God in his goodness and wisdom reveals himself. With deeds and words, he reveals himself and his plan of loving goodness which he decreed from all eternity in Christ. According to this plan, all people by the grace of the Holy Spirit are to share in the divine life as adopted "sons" in the only begotten Son of God. (CCC 50-53, 68-69)

The first stages of God's Revelation

From the very beginning, God manifested to our first parents, Adam and Eve, and invited them to intimate communion with himself. After their fall, he did not cease his revelation to them but promised salvation for all their descendants. After the flood, he made a covenant with Noah, a covenant between himself and all living beings. (CCC 54-55, 70-71)

The next stages of God's Revelation

God chose Abram, calling him out of his country, making him "the father of a multitude of nations" (Gen 17: 5), and promising to bless in him "all the families of the earth" (Gen 12:3). The people descended from Abraham would be the trustee of the divine promise made to the patriarchs. God formed Israel as his chosen people, freeing them from slavery in Egypt, establishing with them the covenant of Mount Sinai, and, through Moses, giving them his Law. The prophets proclaimed a radical redemption of the people and salvation which would include all nations in a new and everlasting covenant. From the people of Israel and from the house of King David, would be born the Messiah, Jesus. (CCC 59-64, 72)

The full and definitive stage of God's Revelation

The full and definitive stage of God's revelation is accomplished in his Word made flesh, Jesus Christ, the mediator and fullness of Revelation. He brings the only- begotten Son of God made man, is the perfect and definitive Word of the Father. In the sending of the Son and the gift of the Spirit, Revelation is now fully complete, although the faith of the Church must gradually grasp its full significance over the course of centuries. (CCC 65-66, 73)

"In giving of his Son, his only and definitive Word, God spoke everything to us at once in this sole Word, and he has no more to say." (Saint John of the Cross)

The value of private revelations

While not belonging to the deposit of faith, private revelations may help a person to live the faith as long as they lead us to Christ. The Magisterium of the Church, which has the duty of evaluating such private revelations, cannot accept those who claim to surpass or correct that definitive Revelation which is Christ. (CCC 67)

THE TRANSMISSION OF DIVINE REVELATION

Divine revelation transmitted

God "desires all men to be saved and to come to the knowledge of the truth" (1 Timothy 2; 24), that is, of Jesus Christ. For this reason, Christ must be proclaimed to all according to his own command, "Go forth and teach all nations" (Matthew 28: 19). And this is brought about by Apostolic Tradition. (CCC 74)

Apostolic tradition

Apostolic Tradition is the transmission of the message of Christ, brought about from the very beginnings of Christianity by means of preaching, bearing witness, institutions, worship, and inspired writings. The Apostles transmitted all they received from Christ and learned from the Holy Spirit to their successors, the bishops, and through them to all generations until the end of the world. (CCC 75-79, 83, 96, 98)

Apostolic Tradition Occur

Apostolic Tradition occurs in two ways: through the living transmission of the word of God (also simply called Tradition) and through Sacred Scripture which is the same proclamation of salvation in written form. (CCC 76)

The relationship between Tradition and Sacred Scripture

Tradition and Sacred Scripture are bound closely together and communicate one with the other. Each of them makes present and fruitful in the Church the mystery of Christ. They flow out of the same divine wellspring and together makeup one sacred deposit of faith from which the Church derives her certainty about revelation. (CCC 80- 82, 97)

The deposit of faith entrusted

The Apostles entrusted the deposit of faith to the whole of the Church. Thanks to its supernatural sense of faith the people of God as a whole, assisted by the Holy Spirit and guided by the magisterium of the Church, never ceases to welcome, penetrate more deeply and live more fully from the gift of divine revelation. (CCC 84, 91, 94, 99)

The task of authentically interpreting the deposit of faith

The task of giving an authentic interpretation of the deposit of faith has been entrusted to the living teaching office of the Church alone, that is, to the successor of Peter, the Bishop of Rome, and to the bishops in communion with him. To this magisterium, which in the service of the Word of God enjoys the certain charism of truth, belongs also to the task of defining dogmas which are formulations of the truths contained in divine Revelation. This authority of the Magisterium also extends to those truths necessarily connected with Revelation. (CCC 85- 90,100)

The relationship between Scripture, Tradition and the Magisterium

Scripture, Tradition, and Magisterium are closely united with each other that one of them cannot stand without the others.

Working together, each in its own way, under the action of the one Holy Spirit, they all contribute effectively to the salvation of souls. (CCC95)

SACRED SCRIPTURE

Sacred Scripture teaches the Truth

Because God himself is the author of Sacred Scripture. For this reason, it is said to be inspired and teach without error those truths which are necessary for our salvation. The Holy Spirit inspired the human authors who wrote what he wanted to teach us. The Christian faith, however, is not a "religion of the Book," but of the Word of God-''not a written and mute word, but incarnate and living "(*Saint Bernard of Clairvaux*). (CCC 105- 108, 135-136

Sacred Scripture to be read

Sacred Scripture must be read and interpreted with the help of the Holy Spirit and under the guidance of the magisterium of the Church according to three criteria: 1) it must be read with attention to the content and unity of the whole of the Scripture; 2) it must be read within the living Tradition of the Church; 3) it must be read with attention to analogy of faith, that is, the inner harmony which exists among the truths of the faith themselves. (CCC 109-119, 137)

The canon of the Scripture

The Canon of Scripture is the complete list of the sacred writings that the Church has come to recognize through Apostolic Tradition. The Canon consist of 46 books of the Old Testament and 27 of the New Testament. (CCC 120, 138)

The importance of the Old Testament for Christians

Christin venerates the Old Testament as the true word of God. All of the books of the Old Testament re divinely inspired and retain a permanent value. They bear witness to the divine pedagogy of God's saving love. They are written, above all, to prepare for the coming of Christ, the Savior of the universe. (CCC 121- 123)

The importance of the New Testament for Christians

The New Testament, whose central object is Jesus Christ, conveys to us the ultimate truth of divine Revelation. Within the

New Testament the four Gospels of Matthew, Luke, and John are the heart of all the Scriptures because they are the principal witness to the life and teaching of Jesus. As such, they hold a unique place in the Church. (CCC 124- 127, 139)

The unity that exists between the Old and the New Testaments

Scripture is one insofar as the Word of God is one. God's plan of salvation is one, and the divine inspiration of both Testaments is one. The Old Testament prepares for the New and the New Testament fulfilled the Old; the two shed light on each other. (CCC 128- 130, 140)

Sacred Scripture plays a vital role in the Life of the Church

Sacred Scripture gives support and vigour to the life of the Church. For the children of the Church, it is a confirmation of the faith, food for the soul and the fount of the spiritual life. Sacred Scripture is the soul of theology and of pastoral preaching. The Psalmist says that it is a lamp to my feet and light to my path (Psalm 119:105). The Church, therefore, exhorts all to read Sacred Scripture frequently because ignorance of the Scripture is ignorance of Christ *(Saint Jerome)*. (CCC 131- 133, 141-142)

The man responds to God who reveals himself

Sustained by divine grace, we respond to God with the obedience of faith, which means the full surrender of ourselves to God and the acceptance of his truth insofar as it is guaranteed by the One who is Truth itself. (CCC 142- 143)

Catechists and youth ministers are called to live the word of God in order to become good and effective evangelizer. As God revealed himself through his words and deeds, human beings and all living creatures are called to live according to what God showed to us. Through his loving goodness, God give his only begotten Son, the Word made flesh to save us and make us adopted sons. Revelation teaches us to share and to give not what we have but who we are, just as our Lord Jesus Christ became one of us, he humbled himself in order to save, his beloved friends, and humanity. One of our responsibility is to proclaim the Word of God in our deeds and words. We must not cease revealing and proclaiming the truth as God want us to do, to go throughout the world and tell the Good News. By giving ourselves without reserves and sharing to others what we have experienced in God's grace is the most important thing that man learns from these themes.

The Reign of God

INTRODUCTION:

After the death of John the Baptist, Jesus came and began his public ministry. He began to preach about the **Kingdom of God which is at hand** and sent out a command, **"repent and believe in the gospel."** (CCC 541). For those who listen to this messiah, the Christ, what he offers to them is the Kingdom of God but in order to accept and receive willingly this Kingdom of God – it entails that they have to repent and believe!

What is this Kingdom of God all about? In the scriptures particularly the New Testament, Jesus who is always seen and seated with the poor, the outcast, and the sinners kept on mentioning that the **Kingdom of God belongs to the poor and the lowly who are humbled of hearts.** (Mt.5:3). And furthermore, these poor and lowly are being described as the **"little ones"** from whom the **Kingdom of God is being revealed.** (Mt 11:25)

DEFINITION OF TERMS:

REIGN OF GOD/KINGDOM OF GOD - "kingship," "kingly rule," "reign" or "sovereignty" is a foundational concept in Christianity, as it is the central theme of Jesus of Nazareth's message in the synoptic Gospels.

THE REIGN OF GOD IN THE FATHER'S PLAN OF CREATION

Although the specific term "kingdom of God" is rare in the Old Testament, the idea which underlies this term is found everywhere: Yahweh, our God, is eternal King and Lord forever and ever. We can find this in Exodus 15 where Yahweh's sovereignty over his people was seen. Also, mentioned several times as King of Israel in Psalms (Cf. Psalm 95, 22, 47) and from the prophets (Cf. Isaiah 33:22).

Understanding the Kingdom of God would direct us to have a clear notion of the **Father's Will**. We have seen and heard the story of how God called a man named Abraham, who made a remarkable decision of following God's commands; and because of his obedience, a promise was given: a nation known as Israel, whom God made a covenant with. (CCC 762) They will be His people and He will be their God (Ex. 6:7); a God who asks for their obedience not for Him in general but for their welfare as they are starting to gather together as one people. Consequently, if they have proven themselves, His blessings will flow to them and to their children.

The Father's will would always involve God and his people. A God who is not so distant but a personal God who always makes sure his presence be felt by his people as seen as a cloud by day and a pillar of fire by night (Ex. 13:21); and the Word made flesh who dwelt among us, full of grace and truth (CCC 423).

We have seen from this perspective not only a personal God but who really made an intimate relationship with his people. Possible questions might arise from these circumstances or situations, such as "What is it for?" Why is it God, who is a perfect and infinite Being, who will meddle in the affairs of a man who is his creation and who is imperfect and finite and have flaws? The Father's will, from this personal intimate relationship, would allow us to understand that He has a plan for us. Ours is a creation different from the rest, being given time by the Father, slowly woven and finally given the breath of life, In His image and likeness (Genesis: Creation story). God freely creates out of sheer love, to share His own divine life and goodness. Creation is the first step in God's plan of salvation for all through Jesus Christ. From this standpoint, **we were raised up and given a share of His divine life!** (CCC 541/LG 2).

THE REIGN OF GOD IN THE HISTORICAL MINISTRY OF JESUS

The Kingdom of God can only be realized through a **gathering of people who recognizes Christ himself as the centre of this gathering!** "Everyone is called to enter the kingdom. First announced to the children of Israel, this messianic kingdom is intended to accept men of all nations. To enter it, one must first accept Jesus' word:

The **WORD OF THE LORD** is compared to a seed that is sown in a field; those who hear it with faith and are numbered among the little flock of Christ have truly received the kingdom. Then, by its own power, the seed sprouts and grows until the harvest.

The kingdom belongs to the poor and lowly, which means those who have accepted it with humble hearts. Jesus is sent to "preach good news to the poor"; he declares them blessed, for "theirs is the kingdom of heaven." To them - the "little ones" the Father is pleased to reveal what remains hidden from the wise and the learned. Jesus shares the life of the poor, from the cradle to the cross; he experiences hunger, thirst and privation. Jesus identifies himself with the poor of every kind and makes active love toward them the condition for entering his kingdom. Jesus invites sinners to the table of the kingdom: "I came not to call the righteous, but sinners."

He invites them to that conversion without which one cannot enter the kingdom, but shows them in **word and deed** his Father's boundless mercy for them and the vast "joy in heaven over one sinner who repents". The supreme proof of his love will be the sacrifice of his own life "for the forgiveness of sins".

Jesus' invitation to enter his kingdom comes in the form of parables, a characteristic feature of his teaching. Through his parables, he invites people to the feast of the kingdom, but he also asks for a radical choice: to gain the kingdom, one must give everything. **Words are not enough, deeds are required.** The parables are like mirrors for man: will he be hard soil or good earth for the word? What use has he made of the talents he has received? Jesus and the presence of the kingdom in this world are secretly at the heart of the parables. One must enter the kingdom, that is, become a disciple of Christ, in order to "know the secrets of the kingdom of heaven". For those who stay "outside", everything remains enigmatic." (CCC 543-546)

"Jesus accompanies his words with many **"MIGHTY WORKS AND WONDERS AND SIGNS"**, which manifest that the kingdom is present in him and attest that he was the promised Messiah. The signs worked by Jesus attest that the Father has sent him. They invite belief in him. To those who turn to him in faith, he grants what they ask. So miracles strengthen faith in the One who does his Father's works; they bear witness that he is the Son of God." (CCC 547-550)

<u>REIGN OF GOD IN THE PERMANENT ACTION OF THE HOLY SPIRIT</u>

In the Lord's Prayer, "thy kingdom come" refers primarily to the final coming of the reign of God through Christ's return. But, far from distracting the Church from her mission in this present world, this desire commits her to it all the more strongly. Since Pentecost, the coming of that Reign is the work of the Spirit of the Lord who "complete(s) his work on earth and brings us the fullness of grace."

"The kingdom of God (is) righteousness and peace and joy in the Holy Spirit." The end-time in which we live is the age of the outpouring of the Spirit. Ever since Pentecost, a decisive battle has been joined between "the flesh" and the Spirit. Only a pure soul can boldly say: "Thy kingdom come." One who has heard Paul say, "Let not sin therefore reign in your mortal bodies," and has purified himself in action, thought and word will say to God: "Thy kingdom come!"

By discernment according to the Spirit, Christians have to distinguish between the growth of the Reign of God and the progress of the culture and society in which they are involved. This distinction is not a separation. Man's vocation to eternal life does not suppress but actually reinforces, his duty to put into action in this world the energies and means received from the Creator to serve justice and peace. (CCC 2818-2820)

<u>REIGN OF GOD IN THE LITURGY</u>

The kingship of God is more of a reign where it is not only a noun but an action noun. This Kingdom of God lies ahead of us and yet is brought to us by the Word incarnate, proclaimed in the Gospel and being highlighted in Christ's death and resurrection. (CCC 2816).

And as we continue to *"remember him" in our* celebration of the Holy Eucharist, we earnestly pray that he may quickly come and rest in us. As Jesus rests in us, this kingdom of God also rests in us. As Jesus resurrects, we also rise up with him. True to God's plan, that we whom He has created and desired to have a share in his divine life, and yet decided to separate and distant ourselves from him through sin. Still faithful to his calling, the Father sent his Son, the Word Incarnate, the Word made flesh for our salvation.

When we pray as we are being led by the Spirit, "may your kingdom of God," we ask for the final coming of the reign of God through Christ's return (Cf. Titus 2:13). Through the working of the Spirit in us, it gave us the graces we need to continue the missionary task being entrusted to us as it did through the experience of the apostles during the Pentecost event.

REIGN OF GOD IN THE MISSION OF THE CHURCH

"The Church is effectively and concretely at the service of the kingdom. This is seen especially in her preaching, which is a call to conversion. **Preaching constitutes the Church's first and fundamental way of serving the coming of the kingdom in individuals and in human society.** Eschatological salvation begins even now in the newness of life in Christ: "To all who believed in him, who believed in his name, he gave the power to become children of God" (Jn 1:12).

The Church, then, serves the kingdom by establishing communities and founding new particular churches, and by guiding them to mature faith and charity in openness toward others, in service to individuals and society, and in understanding and esteem for human institutions.

The Church serves the kingdom by spreading throughout the world the "gospel values" which are an expression of the kingdom and which help people to accept God's plan. It is true that the inchoate reality of the kingdom can also be found beyond the confines of the Church among peoples everywhere, to the extent that they live "gospel values" and are open to the working of the Spirit who breathes when and where he wills (cf. Jn 3:8). But it must immediately be added that this temporal dimension of the kingdom remains incomplete unless it is related to the kingdom of Christ present in the Church and straining towards eschatological fullness.

The many dimensions of the kingdom of God do not weaken the foundations and purposes of missionary activity, but rather strengthen and extend them. The Church is the sacrament of salvation for all mankind, and her activity is not limited only to those who accept her message. She is a dynamic force in mankind's journey toward the eschatological kingdom and is the sign and promoter of gospel values.

The Church contributes to mankind's pilgrimage of conversion to God's plan through her witness and through such activities as dialogue, human promotion, commitment to justice and peace, education and the care of the sick, and aid to the poor and to children. In carrying on these activities, however, she never loses sight of the priority of the transcendent and spiritual realities which are premises of eschatological salvation.

Finally, the Church serves the kingdom by her intercession, since the kingdom by its very nature is God's gift and work, as we are reminded by the gospel parables and by the prayer which Jesus taught us. We must ask for the kingdom, welcome it and make it grow within us; but we must also work together so that it will be welcomed and will grow among all people, until the time when Christ "delivers the kingdom to God the Father" and "God will be everything to everyone" (cf. 1 Cor 15:24, 28). (Redemptoris Missio #20)

PASTORAL APPLICATION

In all aspects of our human life, the reign of God whom we recognize as Jesus Christ should be made present. Mother Teresa of

Calcutta always reminds us to see the face of Jesus in each other, when we do this, we will learn to serve one another from the heart. In doing so, the Kingdom of God has come upon you (Mt. 12:28).

In my vocation of meeting and journeying with the youth who are distracted with so many temporal things that at times difficult for them to see, feel and experience the Reign of God - the Kingdom of God, all the more I ask, through prayer, for the Spirit to guide and strengthen me to be the face of Christ for them. By doing this, I may be able to give them a sense that there is goodness in this world even though they experience hate, anger and indifference in their personal and social relationships. To open up to them about their possibilities by letting them realize that there is a loving Father who cares for them despite all their bad experiences; possibilities as God's gifts once they discover them. It would lead them to live life to the fullest and become the persons they themselves would like to be. In every recollection and retreat, I give is an opportunity for me to let the youth feel the presence and love of God, to enter or renew their relationship with God; and when these youth are touched by God, they may be able to become instruments of God's love, mercy and forgiveness to others. In their mind and heart attuned now to God, they may be able to serve Him by serving others. Youth serving youth...being a beacon of hope and light to others.

This is the invitation of the God to us.... to let his kingdom come into this world. A kingdom of peace, of love, of joy, of peace, and of righteousness. A kingdom where all of us are invited to be a part of. A kingdom once planted by Jesus, continued by his apostles and disciples and now being entrusted to us as our mission.

In a world where anyone can feel and experience uncertainties that leads to anxieties and fears, we are compelled by the Spirit of the Lord, to:

Bring good news to the poor;

He has sent me to proclaim release to captives

And recovery of sight to the blind,

To let the oppressed go free,

To proclaim the year of the Lord's favour.

BOSCO EKKA, SDB

(Lk, 4: 18-19. NRSV)

CHAPTER FOUR

The Trinitarian Life of God

Introduction

This chapter seeks to offer an attempt at presenting the Trinitarian life of God--the Father, Son and Holy Spirit--as understood from theological-pastoral studies under the Master of Religious Studies program of the Don Bosco Center of Studies.

Below is a definition of the terms:

Trinity (Holy Trinity, Blessed Trinity): the central mystery of Christian faith and life, i.e. belief in one God in three divine persons: Father, Son and Holy Spirit. It is the mystery of God in himself; therefore the source of all the other mysteries of faith. It is the most fundamental and essential teaching in the "hierarchy of the truths of faith"[1].

Mystery: a religious belief based on divine revelation, especially one regarded as beyond human understanding.

Communion: sharing or fellowship

Mission: being sent, as in Mt 28:19[2]

Church: "convocation"; designating the assembly of those whom God's Word "convokes," i.e., gathers together to form the People of God, and who themselves, nourished with the Body of Christ, become the Body of Christ[3]; the icon of the Trinity and universal sacrament of salvation **Baptized**: those who receive the Sacrament of Baptism ("I baptize you in the name of the Father, Son and Holy Spirit), thus a sharer in the Trinitarian life of God.

The theme is intended to be presented by first laying down its theological foundations as drawn from both Scriptures and the teachings of the Church, and following it with its significance for today's context for catechetics and youth ministry.

In the Old Testament, Biblical language does not have clear reference to the Trinity; only allusions, e.g. in the use of personification via the words "Spirit", "Word" and "Wisdom", which are manifestations of God's creative and sanctifying power; in the use of the majestic plural (for example, Gen 1:26[4], 3:22[5] and 11:7[6]; and in the texts about the Lord and His messenger, the Spirit of God and divine Wisdom as proceeding from God.

Starting from the Gospels in the New Testament, there are explicit references to the Trinity[7] as well as descriptions, e.g. in the Annunciation, in the Baptism of Jesus, and in his Transfiguration. The Lord Jesus reveals the Father[8], and that the Father and He are one[9]. Jesus is the Logos, who was there in the beginning[10]; he promises another Advocate, the Holy Spirit, sent too by the Father[11]. There is also an abundance of Trinitarian references in the Pauline letters: worthy of mention are the salutations[12] and conclusions[13] with a Trinitarian tone, as well as what could be described as a Trinitarian summary of salvation history[14].

The Church believes the Trinity as "a mystery of the faith in the strict sense, one of the 'mysteries that are hidden in God, which can never be known unless they are revealed by God'"[15].

She affirms that God provided glimpses of his Trinitarian being in salvation history recorded in the Old Testament, but the full revelation of the Trinitarian mystery came through the Incarnation of the Son of God and the sending of the Holy Spirit.

One God in three divine persons, which are distinct from one another. "'God is one but not solitary.'... They are distinct from one another in their relations of origin: 'It is the Father who generates, the Son who is begotten, and the Holy Spirit who proceeds.'"[16], and in the "relationships which relate them to one another: 'In the relational names of the persons the Father is related to the Son, the

Son to the Father, and the Holy Spirit to both. While they are called three persons in view of their relations, we believe in one nature or substance.'... 'Because of that unity the Father is wholly in the Son and wholly in the Holy Spirit; the Son is wholly in the Father and wholly in the Holy Spirit; the Holy Spirit is wholly in the Father and wholly in the

Son.'"[17] "Thus the Church confesses, following the New Testament, 'one God and Father from

whom all things are, and one Lord Jesus Christ, through whom all things are, and one Holy Spirit in whom all things are'"[18].

This revealed truth is at the very root of the life of the Church, primarily in Baptism, as shown in the Baptismal rite, and finds expression in her works of evangelization and catechesis, of charity and of the liturgy[19]. The essential mark of the Christian life, the Trinitarian mystery is codified into the faith of the Church through her Creeds. The Church herself is an "icon" of the Trinity--her being a gathered assembly mirrors the unity of her origin: the Father and Son in the Holy Spirit[20]. God is love[21]--in Him is the communion of the three divine persons--and the Church is a reflection of that loving communion. In the Church too, the ongoing work of creation, redemption and sanctification of the three divine persons continues, making her the universal sacrament of salvation, because "God desires 'that the whole human race may become one

People of God, form one Body of Christ, and be built up into one temple of the Holy Spirit.'"[22] Therefore, each person baptized in the Trinitarian community is called to share in that union: adopted of the Father in Christ, through the Holy Spirit.

In summary, the Trinitarian dogma teaches one God in three divine persons: unity in God, and mutual relation among the three persons. This revealed mystery shows absolute oneness in God and full equality of persons. The Lord Jesus revealed himself as sent by the Father, and the Spirit was sent by the Father and the Son, on a mission of redemption and sanctification out of love for sinful humanity. As such, the Holy Trinity is the central vivifying truth that responds to the deepest longings of the human heart: "By the grace of Baptism 'in the name of the Father and of the Son and of the Holy Spirit, we are called to share in the life of the Blessed Trinity, here on earth in the obscurity of faith, and after death in eternal light"[23].

Significant Pastoral Application

"God is love: Father, Son and Holy Spirit. God freely wills to communicate the glory of his blessed life. Such is the 'plan of his loving-kindness, conceived by the Father before the foundation of the world, in his beloved Son: 'He destined us in love to be his sons' and 'to be conformed to the image of his Son', through 'the spirit of sonship'. This plan is a 'grace [which] was given to us in Christ Jesus before the ages began', stemming immediately from Trinitarian love. It unfolds in the work of creation, the whole history of salvation after the fall, and the missions of the Son and the Spirit, which are continued in the mission of the Church."[24]

Indeed, all the baptized--among them, catechists and youth ministers--are called to deepen, in themselves and in those entrusted to them, what the Church shares into our human lives through Baptism, i.e. the Trinitarian life. As God is a communion of persons, the Church is called to gather humankind and all of creation into a life of communion with one another, coming from the perfect communion which is the Trinity. As the Father, Son and Holy Spirit continue the

work of creation, redemption and sanctification, we too who are baptized in the name of the Triune God are called toward lives of the same purpose and meaningful relationships: "The communion of the Holy Trinity is the source and criterion of truth in every relationship. It is lived out in prayer, above all in the Eucharist... To God, the better offering is peace, brotherly concord, and a people made one in the unity of the Father, Son, and Holy Spirit"[25].

Catechists and youth ministers are called to strengthen and deepen what was celebrated in Christian initiation: the baptizing in the name of the Father and of the Son and of the Holy Spirit should lead to a life lived to the glory of the Triune God: "Hence the whole

Christian life is a communion with each of the divine persons, without in any way separating them. Everyone who glorifies the Father does so through the Son in the Holy Spirit; everyone who follows Christ does so because the Father draws him and the Spirit moves him"[26].

In a specific way, there is a call to prayer, "the living relationship of the children of God with their Father who is good beyond measure, with his Son Jesus Christ and with the Holy Spirit... Thus, the life of prayer is the habit of being in the presence of the thrice-holy God and in communion with him [which is] always possible because, through Baptism, we have already been united with Christ."[27] Prayer, whether in the liturgical assembly or in private, "is always prayer of the Church; it is a communion with the Holy Trinity"[28].

Conclusion

The Trinitarian dogma is meant to be the "deepest source, closest inspiration and the brightest illumination of the meaning of life that we can imagine."[29] When allowed to enlighten, inspire and sharpen ecclesial programs and efforts on catechetics and youth ministry, the Christian faith in the Trinitary--in the Father, Son and Holy Spirit--can be truly formative in the lives of people: both here on earth and in view of the life to come.

O my God, Trinity whom I adore, help me forget myself entirely so to establish myself in you, unmovable and peaceful as if my soul were already in eternity.

May nothing be able to trouble my peace or make me leave you, O my unchanging God, but may each minute bring me more deeply into your mystery!

Grant my soul peace.

Make it your heaven, your beloved dwelling and the place of your rest. May I never abandon you there, but may I be there, whole and entire, completely vigilant in my faith,

entirely adoring,

and wholly given over to your creative action.

(Prayer to the Most Holy Trinity by St. Elizabeth of the Trinity,
a Carmelite nun)
The grace of the Lord Jesus Christ and the love of God
and the fellowship of the Holy Spirit be with you all.

❧❧❧

1 Cf. CCC 234.

2 "Go, therefore, and make disciples of all nations, baptizing them in the name of the Father, and of the Son, and of the Holy Spirit..."

3 Cf. CCC 777.

4 "Then God said: Let us make human beings in our image, after our likeness."

5 "Then the Lord God said: See! The man has become like one of us, knowing good and evil!"

6 "Come, let us go down and there confuse their language so that no one will understand the speech of another."

7 For example, Mt 28:19.

8 "No one knows the Son except the Father, and no one knows the Father except the Son and anyone to whom the Son wishes to reveal him" (Mt 11:27).

9 "The Father and I are one." (Jn 10:30).

10 "In the beginning was the Word, and the Word was with God, and the Word was God." (Jn 1:1).

11 "And I will ask the Father, and he will give you another Advocate to be with you always, the Spirit of truth." (Jn 14:16).

12 For example: "...the gospel about his Son, descended from David according to the flesh, but established as Son of God in power according to the spirit of holiness through resurrection from the dead, Jesus Christ our Lord." (Rom 1:3-4).

13 For example: "The grace of the Lord Jesus Christ and the love of God and the fellowship of the holy Spirit be with all of you." (2 Cor 13:13).

[14] "But when the fullness of time had come, God sent his Son, born of a woman, born under the law, to ransom those under the law, so that we might receive adoption. As proof that you are children, God sent the spirit of his Son into our hearts, crying out, 'Abba, Father!'" (Gal 4:4-6).

[15] CCC 237.

[16] CCC 254.

[17] CCC 255.

[18] CCC 258.

[19] Cf. CCC 249.

[20] Cf. CCC 813.

[21] 1 Jn 4:8.

[22] CCC 776.

[23] CCC 265.

[24] CCC 257.

[25] CCC 2845.

[26] CCC 259.

[27] CCC 2565.

[28] CCC 2655.

[29] Attributed to Leonardo Boff.

The Paschal Mystery of Jesus

Definition of Terms:

Easter- A feast that commemorates Christ's resurrection and is observed with variations of date due to different calendars on the first Sunday after the paschal full moon.

Passion- The sufferings of Christ between the night of the Last Supper and His death

Death- The end of life: the time when someone or something dies the ending of a particular person's life. The permanent end of something that is not alive: the ruin or destruction of something.

Mystery- in the Biblical sense is understood as realities and truths of God's salvific plan which we can understand by God's revelation.

The Paschal mystery

The Paschal mystery is the passion, death, resurrection, and glorification of Jesus, and "stands at the centre of the Christian faith because God's saving plan was accomplished once for all by the redemptive death of his Son Jesus Christ." (Compendium of the Catechism of the Catholic Church 112; see also CCC 571-573)

The word "paschal" came from the Greek πασχα (pascha), which is derived from Hebrew פֶּסַח (pesach), which means "the passing over" (See Ex 12:13, 23, 27 and Is 31:5).[1]

The Paschal mystery is a historical event, i.e., did it really happen

The Paschal mystery of Jesus is a historical event, i.e., it is an event that actually happened in a specific place and time, within a particular culture, and was witnessed by hundreds, even thousands, of people. There are written documents--both biblical and non-biblical accounts--that recorded the events of Jesus' passion, crucifixion, and death and could attest to the historicity of this event. For the biblical accounts, we have the four canonical Gospels: Matthew, Mark, Luke, and John. For non-biblical accounts, one can refer to the writings of the Jewish historian Josephus Flavius; the Roman politicians Suetonius, Tacitus, and Pliny the Younger; and the pagan Mara bar Serapion. One may also refer to the apocryphal writing *The Protoevangelium of James*.

"Jesus' sufferings took their historical, concrete form from the fact that he was 'rejected by the elders and the chief priests and the scribes,' who handed 'him to the Gentiles to be mocked and scourged and crucified.'" (CCC 572; see Mk 8:31 and Mt 20:19 for the Biblical quotation)

Jesus really rise from the dead

The Christian faith teaches that "on the third day He rose again from the dead." This event in human history is now known as the Resurrection of Jesus or simply the Resurrection. It is "the crowning truth of our faith in Christ, a faith believed and lived as the central truth by the first Christian community; handed on as fundamental by Tradition; established by the documents of the New Testament, and preached as an essential part of the Paschal mystery along with the cross." (CCC 638)

In his first letter to the Corinthians, St. Paul said, "I delivered to you as of first importance what I also received, that Christ died for our sins in accordance with the scriptures, and that he was buried, that he was raised on the third day in accordance with the scriptures, and that he appeared to Cephas, then to the Twelve" (1 Cor 15:3-4). This passage from the Corinthians verifies that the Resurrection of our Lord is a real, historical event, with manifestations that were historically verified.

There are three undeniable proofs that Jesus rose from the dead. The first proof is the empty tomb. CCC 640 teaches that "the first element we encounter in the framework of the Easter events is the empty tomb." However, in itself, it is not a direct proof of Jesus' Resurrection since the absence of the Body of Christ can be explained otherwise. "Nonetheless the empty tomb was still an essential sign for all. Its discovery by the disciples was the first step toward recognizing the very fact of the Resurrection. This was the case, first with the holy women, and then with Peter. The disciple 'whom Jesus loved' affirmed that when he entered the empty tomb and discovered 'the linen cloths lying there,' 'he saw and believed.' This suggests that he realized from the empty tomb's condition that the absence of Jesus' body could not have been of human doing and that Jesus had not simply returned to earthly life as had been the case with Lazarus." (CCC 640)

If the empty tomb is not a direct proof of the Resurrection, then how can one be assured that it actually happened? The answer lies in the second proof: Eyewitnesses' accounts. According to St. Paul, Jesus appeared to Peter, the Twelve, to five hundred people at once (some, according to St. Paul, were still alive at the time of his writing), to James, to all the apostles, and lastly, to him (see 1 Cor 15:3-8). Now, sceptics say that the witnesses were just hallucinating and we're actually seeing an illusion or vision. However, a modern study in the field of psychology proves that hallucination does not work this way.[2]

The appearance to the disciples made them proclaim this event to others, gaining others to follow in this faith, eventually giving rise to a movement--the Christian movement. This is the third proof: the explosion of Christianity. After Jesus rose from the dead and ascended into heaven, there was a huge number of people who suddenly accepted the proclamation or news that was handed to them. Eventually, there was a new movement that was happening-- a new religion arising. What is surprising is that those who proclaimed it underwent persecution, torture, and even death. If it were a lie, they would have not gone as far as dying for this belief.

The Paschal mystery a mystery of faith

"Mystery" is a word that one usually uses when one refers to something that is outside the full comprehension of the human mind. However, in Biblical language, "mystery" has a deeper meaning. It refers to the aspects of God's plan of salvation for mankind (See Am 3:7; Is 21:28; Dan 2:27-45).

The term "mystery of faith," in theology, is an article of faith or doctrine which defies man's ability to grasp it fully and transcends reason.[3]

The Paschal mystery is a mystery of faith because it "stands at the centre of the Good News that the apostles, and the Church following them, are to proclaim to the world. God's saving plan was accomplished 'once for all by the redemptive death of his Son Jesus Christ" (CCC 571). This, however, cannot be fully grasped by human comprehension and transcends human reason, making it to be a mystery just like the dogma of the Trinity.

The Paschal mystery is the core of life and the Christian proclamation

The Paschal mystery--the Passion, Death, and most especially the Resurrection of Jesus Christ--was the turning point in human history and ultimately the basis of the Christian faith. The preaching of the Apostles is centred on it. St. Paul said, "if Christ has not been raised, then empty [too] is our preaching; empty, too, your faith. Then we are also false witnesses to God because we testified against God that he raised Christ" (1 Cor 15:14-15). The whole of Christianity is based on this event. If it did not happen, especially the Resurrection, then our faith is based on a lie.

The Paschal mystery is so important that St. Peter declared that the character of an Apostle was to be a witness to it. When the Apostles and other disciples were gathered to select someone that would replace Judas, St. Peter made it a requirement that the one to replace Judas must be a witness to it (see Acts 1:22). St. Paul also made many references in his writings the Apostles' preaching of the Resurrection (see Acts 3:15; 4:10; 5:30; 10:40; 13:30 ff.; 17:31; 1 Cor 15; Rom 6:4-5; and 1 Th 1:10).

The Passion, Death, and Resurrection of Jesus is the core of life because as St. Peter said in Acts 1:22, one must be a witness to it. Our Christian faith proclaims that Jesus "suffered, was crucified, died, was buried, and on the third day rose again." If this is our belief, then it follows that our actions, i.e., our way of life, must conform to this belief. Our life must be centred and must revolve around this mystery of our faith.

The Paschal mystery in the liturgy

The Paschal Mystery is at the very heart of Catholic Christian life, liturgy, and spirituality. It is celebrated and made present in the liturgy of the Church, especially the Eucharist which renews the Pascal Sacrifice of Christ as the sacrifice offered by the Church (CCC 1067). In the Liturgy of the Eucharist, it is His own paschal mystery that Christ signifies and makes present. By giving the Holy Spirit he entrusted to them and their successors the power to make present the work of salvation through the Eucharistic sacrifice and the sacraments in which he himself acts to communicate his grace to the faithful of all times and places throughout the world. It is the source and summit of ecclesial life for in the Eucharist is contained the whole spiritual good of the Church, the efficacious sign and sublime cause of that communion with God in the divine life and that unity of the People of God (CCC 1324-1325). Paschal Mystery is celebrated every Sunday and particularly during Triduum Paschal.

The Paschal mystery pastorally

Be acutely aware that in the Mass, the risen Jesus makes present, through sacramental signs, "the bloody sacrifice of the cross" (Trent; CCC 1366) and his victorious resurrection. Active participation, promoted by Vatican II, actually means "greater awareness of the mystery being celebrated and its relationship to daily life." (S Caritatis 52) "In your mind's eye transport yourself to Calvary." (St. Padre Pio) "Offering the immaculate Victim [Jesus wounded on the cross], not only through the hands of the priest but also together with him, they should learn to make an offering of themselves." (Vat II, SC 48) Imagine and love Jesus as Mary saw him bleeding on the cross. And during Communion with the risen Jesus, rejoice with her and live a cheerful life of love of saving people.

There is hope. The Paschal mystery is a great attestation that Jesus became man and was one with us. This gives us assurance that God understands our sufferings because He Himself has experienced them. To put the Paschal mystery in a pastoral way means to share in the sufferings of others, just as our Lord has shared in our suffering. We must let others know and feel that they are not alone in their hardships and trials, that we, too, suffer when they suffer, and that they could share with us their sufferings.

The Paschal mystery also teaches us to endure in our suffering, just as our Lord has endured in His. One of our duties as bearers of the Gospel is to endure. We must help one another in during the different tribulations life offers us. We must continue to cling to hope that behind each suffering is rejoicing. And I believe that is the most important lesson one can learn from the Paschal mystery-- there is hope!

A life lived in obedience to the will of The Father will be rewarded. The passion and death of Jesus were the wills of The Father and Jesus faithfully obeyed it. God the Father did not waste that obedience and saw the trust of Jesus. Hence His intervention was seen in the resurrection of Jesus Christ. The Paschal Mystery is proof that when we seek and obey the will of the Father we will have our own resurrection.

❧❧❧

[1]See https://en.wikipedia.org/wiki/ Paschal_mystery#Etymology_of_'Paschal'.

[2]See https://en.wikipedia.org/wiki/Hallucination and http://www.medicaldaily.com/inside-minds-eye-what-happens-your-brain-when-you-hallucinate-319060.

[3]See https://en.wikipedia.org/wiki/The_mystery_of_faith.

CHAPTER SIX

Divine Filiation

I. Introduction

This chapter aims to explain our divine filiation through the incarnation of Jesus Christ who "became man so that man could become God."

Definitions of Terms:

Trinitarian: The mystery of the Most Holy Trinity is the central mystery of the Christian faith and of the Christian life. God alone can make it known to us by revealing himself as Father, Son and Holy Spirit.[1]

Divine filiation is the condition of being a child of God, and thus a sharer in the life and role of Jesus Christ, who is the Son of God and Redeemer of all men, according to Christian doctrine.[2]

Capax Dei: (Latin phrase) capable of receiving God.

The theme will be developed in three points. And all the dimensions of divine filiation will flow in these three. As we journey and develop the theme, we will discuss it first through the theological point of view with the guidance of scriptural foundation and the Church's teaching or Magisterium and last is the significant pastoral applications.

II. Development of the Divine Filiation

"God became man so that man could become God" is one of the best-known quotes of St. Athanasius in his treatise *On the Incarnation.* It is also quoted in the Catechism of the Catholic Church number 460. By becoming children of God in Jesus we become like him, become Jesus and God. Vatican II states about

Trinity's plan of making human persons as his children in creation and redemption in Lumen Gentium,

In the beginning, God made human nature one and decreed that all his children, scattered as they were, would finally be gathered together as one. It was for this purpose that God sent His Son, whom he appointed heir of all things, that be might be teacher, king and priest of all, the head of the new and universal people of the sons of God. For this too God sent the Spirit of His Son as Lord and Life-giver. It is he who brings together the whole Church and each and every one of those who believe, and who is the well-spring of their unity in the teaching of the apostles and in fellowship, in the breaking of bread and in prayers.[3]

"Children of the Father" in his will from the beginning: Work of creation

The Trinity is the communion of love: the Father is the source of love; the Son is the expression of love and the Spirit is the power of love. It is impossible to see the Son without the Spirit and no one can approach the Father without the Son. From the beginning, the One and Triune God in a communion of love among the Father, the Son and the Holy Spirit has created the whole creation. God created all things good and beautiful.[4] Especially before creating human persons God was in a conversation among themselves, "God said, 'Let us make man in our own image, in the likeness of ourselves'... God created man in the image of himself, in the image of God he created him, male and female he created them" (Gn 1: 26 - 27). Saint Paul in the letter to the Colossians tells us that Jesus is the true image of God, "He is the image of the unseen God, the first-born of all creation, for in him were created all things in heaven and on earth" (Cl 1:15). We are conformed to Jesus.

God created the human person as the summit of the creation not only very good but also in his image and likeness with Capax Dei, the capacity of God which makes us capable to desire God, knowing, receiving and loving him. Moreover, man has the capacity to be like God, to act like him, to cooperate with him in his creation and later on in his redemption. Being in God's image and likeness also means being his children. We are called to the divine filiation to enter into a filial relationship with God which implies righteousness, holiness, and integrity. This is our supreme dignity, children of God the Father.

God gives Adam and Eve freedom and reason to be stewards of his creation including themselves. But because of pride and disobedience, they failed in their stewardship. The Capax Dei comes from God and it only has its meaning in relationship with God. But man was "seduced by the devil, he wanted to 'be like God', but 'without God, before God, and not in accordance with God'."[5] Adam and Eve fell and turned away from God their Creator yet they still remained children of God but became prodigal children, scattered from the house with sweetness and happiness of the Father.

The prodigal "children of the Father": the Fall and sin

After the Fall of the first parents, sin entered the picture of creation together with suffering and death, "all men are implicated in Adam's sin, as St. Paul affirms: 'By one man's disobedience many (that is, all men) were made sinners': 'sin came into the world through one man and death through sin, and so death spread to all men

because all men sinned."[6] Sin is understood "as humanity's rejection of God and opposition to him, even as it continues to weigh heavy on human life and history."[7]

Vatican II talks about the consequences of sin; it makes us have inclinations toward evil. Man has disrupted also his proper relationship to his own ultimate goal as well as his whole relationship toward himself and others and all created things. Man is split within himself and always in a struggle between good and evil, between light and darkness. He is incapable of battling the assaults of evil successfully so that everyone feels as though he is bound by chains.[8]

"By our first parents' sin, the devil has acquired a certain domination over man, even though man remains free. Original sin entails 'captivity under the power of him who thenceforth had the power of death, that is, the devil'."[9] Sin makes the person a slave, "In all truth, I tell you, everyone who commits sin is a slave" (Jn 8: 34).

"Children of the Father" through faith in Jesus and in the Spirit: Work of redemption

God is always faithful. He did not stop loving mankind although we sinned against him but continued his loving plan of salvation. Therefore Jesus was sent as "the lamb of God that takes away the sin of the world" (Jn 1: 29), and as "the 'New Adam' who, because he 'became obedient unto death, even death on a cross', makes amends superabundantly for the disobedience, of Adam."[10] The only Son of the Father was sent into the world and became man to save and free us from sin and restore the divine filiation to mankind, "The Word became flesh, he lived among us" (Jn 1: 14) and "to those who did accept him he gave power to become children of God, to those who believed in his name who were born not from human stock or human desire or human will but from God himself" (Jn 1: 12). Saint Paul also writes in his letter to the Galatians, "When the completion of the time came, God sent his Son, born of a woman, born a subject of the Law, to redeem the subjects of the Law, so that we could receive adoption as sons. As you are sons, God has sent into our hearts the Spirit of his Son crying, 'Abba, Father'" (Gl 4: 4 – 6). "Jesus Christ is true God and true man, in the unity of his divine person; for this reason, he is the one and only mediator between God and men."[11] Vatican II affirms strongly Christ is our only Savior, "Christ, who died and was raised up for all, can through his Spirit offer man the light and the strength to measure up to his supreme destiny. Nor has any other name under the heaven been given to man by which it is fitting for him to be saved."[12] He "restores the divine likeness which had been disfigured from the first sin onward."[13]

Sonship with the Father is a gift from God freely given to us out of love, "You must see what great love the Father has lavished on us by letting us be called God's children – which is what we are!" (1 Jn 3: 1). And we receive it through faith in Jesus, "for all of you are the children of God, through faith, in Christ Jesus" (Gl 3: 26). Through faith in Jesus and the power of the Holy Spirit, we become children of the Father, "All who are guided by the Spirit of God are sons of God; for what you received was not the spirit of slavery to bring you back into fear; you received the Spirit of adoption, enabling us to cry out, 'Abba, Father! The Spirit himself joins with our spirit to bear witness that we are children of God" (Rm 8: 14 - 16).

Faith has been received and handed on in the Church and carried on and given to those who with goodwill, seek the good and truth so that they might also become children of the Father. They will start a new life, the life of children of God in the Spirit without sin, "No one who remains in him sins" (1 Jn 3: 6) and "No one who is a child of God sins because God's seed remains in him. Nor can he sin, because he is a child of God" (1 Jn 3: 9). In the Church he receives and lives his faith and participates in the worship through the liturgy, especially in the sacraments, "Thus by baptism men are plunged into the paschal mystery of Christ: they die with him, are buried with him, and rise with him; they receive the spirit of adoption as sons 'in which we cry: Abba, Father', and thus become true adorers whom the Father seeks."[14] And "all who are made sons of God by faith and baptism should come together to praise God in the midst of his Church, to take part in the sacrifice, and to eat the Lord's Supper."[15]

The life of children of God has to be filled with love, love for God and love for one another, "I give you a new commandment: love one another; you must love one another just as I have loved you" (Jn 13: 34). "I have loved you just as the Father has loved me. Remain in love. If you keep my commandments you will remain in my love, just as I have kept my Father's commandments and remain in his love" (Jn 15: 9 - 10). Because "anyone who loves his brother remains in the light and there is in him nothing to make him fall away" (Jn 2: 10). Besides the relationships of love with God and others, human beings also have a relationship with the world as stewards of God to all creation. The encyclical Laudato si': "On Care For Our Common Home" by Pope Francis reminds us that "human life is grounded in three fundamental and closely intertwined relationships: with God, with our neighbour and with the earth itself."[16] and "Everything is related, and we human beings are united as brothers and sisters on a wonderful pilgrimage, woven together by the love God has for each of his creatures and which also unites us in fond affection with brother sun, sister moon, brother river and mother earth."[17] Therefore we have to take good care of mother earth and all creatures in our daily life.

To end the development of the theme, I quote from the Catechism of the Catholic Church,

The Word became flesh to make us "partakers of the divine nature": "For this is why the Word became man, and the Son of God became the Son of man: so that man, by entering into communion with the Word and thus receiving divine sonship, might become a son of God." "For the Son of God became man so that we might become God." "The only-begotten Son of God, wanting to make us sharers in his divinity, assumed our nature, so that he, made man, might make men gods."[18]

III. Significant Pastoral Application

This is the significance of divine filiation, the fundamental for the Christian life. Once we become His beloved children, we must live out the spirit and fruit of our Christian Initiations through our day to day life. We are not only God's children in name or in our baptismal certificate, but we must also strive to be "God's imitators as beloved children, and walk-in love"[19] manifested in our thoughts, words and actions by following the example of Jesus Christ.

"The joy of the Gospel fills the hearts and lives of all who encounter Jesus".[20] Pope Francis enlightens us that for those who encountered Jesus, this good news of joy will be shared with others. But he also invited us to "renewed our personal encountered with Jesus".[21] We can make this happen through our genuine and constant "contemplative prayer as a prayer of the child of God".[22] "...to gather into one the children of God who are scattered abroad" (Jn 11:52). As a catechist and youth ministers, we are all Christ, anointed to be **signs and bearers of the love of God for the young people**[23]especially "those who are scattered" – poor, abandoned and astray. In spite of our weaknesses or even our good status in life, we must humbly and delightful to serve others without any self-entitlement and expecting in return. Because what we do for others especially the least, we do it for Jesus. And when the time has come, the children of the Father back to his home. May the Lord Jesus welcome us, "Come, you who are blessed by my Father" (Mt 25:34).

Conclusion

Christians are said to be children of God because through divine grace they share in the nature of God. Our divine filiations are not only a title that we are the children of the living and loving God, but first of all, the Holy Trinity – the love of the Father, Jesus and the Holy Spirit embrace us, accept us, love us first since at the beginning. May the example of Mary, the beloved daughter of God, be our inspiration on how we live and to be blessed children of God.

❧❧❧

[1] Catechism of the Catholic Church (1994) no. 261

[2]http://primacyofreason.blogspot.com/2007/09/divine-filiation.html

[3]Vatican II, *Lumen Gentium* (21 November 1964), no. 13.

[4] See Genesis 1

[5]Catechism of the Catholic Church (1992), no. 398.

[6]Ibid., no. 402.

[7]Ibid., no. 386.

[8]See Vatican II, *GaudiumetSpes* (7 December 1965), no. 13.

[9]Ibid., no. 407.

[10]Catechism of the Catholic Church (1992), no. 411.

[11]Catechism of the Catholic Church (1992), no. 480.

[12]Vatican II, *GaudiumetSpes* (7 December 1965), no. 10.

[13]Ibid., no. 22.

[14]Vatican II, *Sacrosanctum Concilium* (4 December 1963), no. 6.

[15]Ibid., no.10.

[16] Pope Francis, The *Encyclical Laudato Si'*(24 May 2015), no 66.

[17] Pope Francis, The *Encyclical Laudato Si'*(24 May 2015), no 92.

[18]Catechism of the Catholic Church (1992), no. 460.

[19] Catechism of the catholic Church (1994), no. 1694.

[20] Pope Francis, Evangelii Gaudium (2013), no.1.

[21] Ibid, no. 3.

[22] Catechism of the Catholic Church (1994), no. 2712.

[23] Constitution and Regulations of the Society of St. Francis of Sales (1984), 2, 47.

CHAPTER SEVEN

The Church

INTRODUCTION

The Holy Spirit, whom Christ the head pours on his members, builds, animates and sanctifies the Church. The Church is the sacrament of the Holy Trinity's communion with men (CCC 747). One, holy catholic, and apostolic are the four essential features of the church. They do not belong to the Church but to Christ, who makes the Church one, holy, Catholic, and apostolic (CCC 811). The Spirit gives the Church mission to proclaim and establish the Kingdom of God among all peoples (CCC 768).

DEFINITION OF TERMS

Ecclesia- Latin word for Church which came from the Greek word "ek-ka-lein" which means "to call out of "means a convocation or an assembly. (CCC 551)

Church- refers to the people of God whom God calls and gathers together from every part of the earth. They form the assembly of those who through faith and Baptism have become children of God, members of Christ's body and temples of the Holy Spirit. (Compendium CCC 147)

THEOLOGICAL, CATECHETICAL AND PASTORAL VIEWPOINT

The Church is considered to be the living work of the Spirit

On the day of Pentecost when the seven weeks of Easter had come to an end, Christ's Passover is fulfilled in the outpouring of the Holy Spirit. Those who were gathered together were filled with the Holy Spirit and began to speak in different tongues, as the Spirit enabled them to proclaim. They proclaim to all people the kingdom Christ himself proclaimed. By the coming of the Holy Spirit, the world was able to enter into the time of the Church. (cf. Acts 2:4, CCC 731,732)

The gifts of the Holy Spirit to the Church

These four characteristics, inseparably linked with each other, indicate special features of the Church and its mission. The Church does not possess them herself; it is Christ who, through the Holy Spirit, makes his Church one, holy, catholic and apostolic, and it is he who calls her to realize each of these qualities. (CCC 811)

The Church is one because she has as her source and exemplar of the unity of the Trinity of Persons in one God. As her Founder and Head, Jesus Christ re-established the unity of all people in one body. As her soul, the Holy Spirit unites all the faithful in communion with Christ. The Church has but one faith, one sacramental life, one apostolic succession, one common hope, and the same charity (cf. Ephesians 4:3-5; Compendium CCC161)

The church is holy in so far as the Most Holy God is her author. Christ has given himself for her to sanctify her and make her a source of sanctification (cf. LG 39). The Holy Spirit gives her life with charity. In the Church, one finds the fullness of the means of salvation. Holiness is the vocation of each of her members and the purpose of all her activities (cf. SC 10). The Church counts among her members the Virgin Mary and numerous Saints who are her models and intercessors. The holiness of the Church is the fountain of sanctification for her children who here on earth recognize themselves as sinners ever in need of conversion and purification (Compendium CCC 165)

The Church is Catholic, that is universal, insofar as Christ is present in her: "Where there is Christ Jesus, there is the Catholic Church" (St. Ignatius of Antioch). The Church proclaims the fullness and the totality of faith; she bears and administers the fullness of the means of salvation; she is sent out by Christ on a mission to the whole human race (Mt.28:19). She is a "missionary of her very nature"(AG 2)

The Church is apostolic in its origin because it has been built on the "foundation of the Apostle" (Ephesians 2:20). She is apostolic in her teaching which is the same as that of the Apostles. She is apostolic by reason of her structure in so far as she is taught, sanctified, and guided until Christ returns by the Apostles through their successors who are the bishops in communion with the successor of Peter (cf.Mt.16:18-19).

THE MISSION OF THE CHURCH ON EARTH

The mission of the Church is to proclaim and establish the Kingdom of God begun by Jesus Christ among all peoples. The Church constitute on earth the seed and beginning of this salvific Kingdom (Compendium CCC150)

The people of God participate in Christ's priestly office in so far as the baptized are consecrated by the Holy Spirit to offer spiritual sacrifices. They share in Christ's prophetic office when with a supernatural sense of faith they adhere unfailingly to that faith and deepen their understanding and witness to it. The people of God share in his kingly office by means of service, imitating Jesus Christ who is the king of the universe and made himself the servant of all, especially the poor and the suffering. (Compendium CCC 153-155)

PASTORAL IMPLICATION

I was incorporated into Christ through baptism therefore part of the people of God. Receiving the gifts of the Spirit I received the charism as a gift, which I can use to serve my fellow men. As a member of the Body of Christ, I am able to share in the threefold mission of Jesus as priest, prophet and king. The characteristic of the Church as one, holy, catholic and Apostolic must be also lived in our day-to-day work and be thought to the people we deal with every day. Being in communion all the members of the church must bear fruit and work hard towards a common goal which is holiness. Every member is called to be an intercessor of all the other members, therefore each one prays for one another's need to achieve the sole destination which is heaven. The presence of each one reminds us of the Kingdom of God proclaimed by God.

DIAGRAM

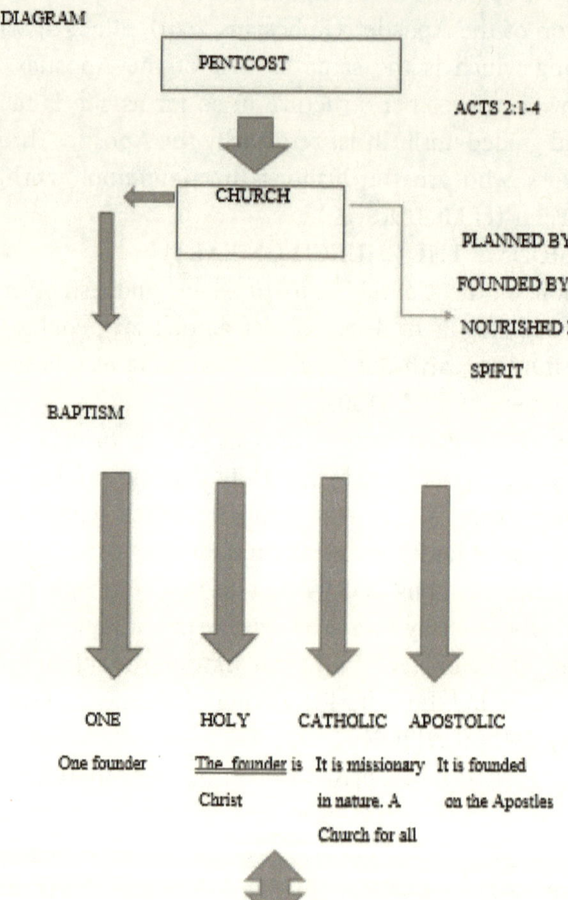

IT IS THE MISSION OF THE CHURCH TO PROCLAIM THE KINGDOM
ANNOUNCED BEFOREHAND BY CHRIST. Mt.28:16-20

Structure of The Church

CHAPTER EIGHT

The Holy Eucharist

Definition of terms

Eucharist:

(a) The Greek word "Eucharist" means "thanksgiving".

(b) The word "Eucharist" is used to refer to the whole service of the mass and especially for the second part, which follows the celebration of the Word of God, reaches its high point with the consecration of the bread and wine into the body and blood of Christ, and ends with communion.

(c) "Eucharist" also refers to Christ's real presence under the appearance of bread and wine.

(d) The "Eucharist" is the greatest of the sacraments and the centre of Church life; it is instituted by Christ at the last supper.

Eucharist is a sacrifice of praise and thanksgiving, in which Christ is present as priest and victim; it represents the new covenant effected through Christ's death and resurrection that reconciled us with God, and (it) anticipates the consummation of the divine kingdom.

Eucharist is a meal: it makes us guests at God's own banquet and expresses our deepest unity in the church.

Eucharist as sacrifice and meal: it efficaciously symbolizes the self-sacrificing service of others to which Christians are called.

Anamnesis (=remembrance; memorial): The bringing to mind of God's saving interventions in history, especially in Christ's passion, death, resurrection and glorification. In the Eucharist, the Lord's command "do this in memory of me" invites the assembly to appropriate the salvation he has effected once and for all.

Mystery of faith: A mystery which surpasses our understanding and can only be received in faith, as in Jn 20:29[1]

Paschal Sacrifice: It refers to Christ's death that accomplishes the definitive redemption of men, through "the Lamb of God, who takes away the sin of the world[2]

Eschatology: literally, "eschatology" means "knowledge of the last things". It is that branch of theology that studies God's final kingdom (FULFILLMENT OF GOD'S REIGN). Eschatology may also be defined as the study of the ULTIMATE FULFILLMENT and MEANING of all CREATION and particularly of HUMANITY in GOD.

Eschatological summit, thus, refers to that ULTIMATE FULFILLMENT of humanity and all creation.

The Eucharist as eschatological summit: this phrase claims that the Eucharist anticipates the ultimate fulfilment of the world, i.e., the sharing of all humanity and creation in Christ's resurrection and glorification.

Eucharist as <u>Memorial</u>

"Then he took the bread, said the blessing, broke it, and gave it to them, saying, "This is my body, which will be given for you; do this in memory of me."[3]

The Eucharist is the memorial of Christ's Passover, the making present and the sacramental offering of his unique sacrifice, in the liturgy of the Church which is his Body. In all the Eucharistic Prayers we find after the words of the institution a prayer called the anamnesis or memorial.[4]

In the sense of Sacred Scripture the memorial is not merely the recollection of past events but the proclamation of the mighty works wrought by God for men. In the liturgical celebration of these events, they become in a certain way present and real. This is how Israel understands its liberation from Egypt: every time Passover is celebrated, the Exodus events are made present to the memory of believers so that they may conform their lives to them.[5]

In the New Testament, the memorial takes on a new meaning. When the Church celebrates the Eucharist, she commemorates Christ's Passover (passion, death, resurrection and glorification), and it is made present, the sacrifice Christ offered once and for all on the cross remains ever-present. "As often as the sacrifice of the Cross by which 'Christ our Pasch has been sacrificed is celebrated on the altar, the work of our redemption is carried out."[6]

Eucharist as *Mystery of Faith*

The Eucharist is truly a great mystery! A mystery 'incomprehensible' to the human mind, but so full of light to the eyes of faith! In fact, for the believers, even if nothing has changed outwardly, the bread is no longer what it was before: it has become the Body of Christ. Its profound being – its substance – is changed. The bread retains the quality of food and the wine that of drink, but actually, Christ is there to communicate himself as food and drink.[7]

The consecration of the bread and wine effects the change of the whole substance of the bread into the substance of the body of Christ our Lord, and of the whole substance of the wine into the substance of his blood. And the holy Catholic Church has fittingly and properly called this change transubstantiation. Truly, the Eucharist is a mysterium fidei, a mystery that surpasses our understanding and can only be received in faith.[8]

Eucharist as *Paschal Sacrifice*

Because it is the memorial of Christ's Passover, the Eucharist is also a sacrifice. The sacrificial character of the Eucharist is manifested in the very words of the institution: "This is my body which is given for you" and "This cup which is poured out for you is the New Covenant in my blood."[9] In the Eucharist, Christ gives us the very body which he gave up for us on the cross, the very blood which he "poured out for many for the forgiveness of sins."[10]

Eucharist as *Eschatological summit*

If the Eucharist is the memorial of the Passover of the Lord Jesus, if by our communion at the altar we are filled "with every heavenly blessing and grace," then the Eucharist is also an anticipation of the heavenly glory.[11]

For in the Eucharist we also receive the pledge of our bodily resurrection at the end of the world: "He who eats my flesh and drinks my blood has eternal life, and I will raise him up at the last day."[12]

Every time this mystery is celebrated, "the work of our redemption is carried on" and we "break the one bread that provides the medicine of immortality, the antidote for death, and the food that makes us live forever in Jesus Christ."[13]

Eucharist as _Grace and Summit of the Life of the Ecclesial Community_

The Eucharist is "the source and summit of the Christian life." "The other sacraments, and indeed all ecclesiastical ministries and works of the apostolate, are bound up with the Eucharist and are oriented toward it. For in the blessed Eucharist is contained the whole spiritual good of the Church, namely Christ himself, our Pasch."[14]

"The Eucharist is the efficacious sign and sublime cause of that communion in the divine life and that unity of the People of God by which the Church is kept in being. It is the culmination both of God's action sanctifying the world in Christ and of the worship, men offer to Christ and through him to the Father in the Holy Spirit."[15]

The unity of the Mystical Body: the Eucharist makes the Church. Those who receive the Eucharist are united more closely to Christ. Through it, Christ unites them to all the faithful in one body - the Church.[16]

The Christian life is expressed in fulfilling the greatest commandment, that is to say in the love of God and neighbour, and this love finds its source in the Blessed Sacrament, which is commonly called the sacrament of love. The Eucharist recalls, makes presents and brings about this charity.[17]

Significant Pastoral Application

Every catechist or youth minister must set the Eucharist at the centre of his/her personal life and community life: love the

Eucharist, adore the Eucharist and celebrate it, especially on Sundays, the Lord's Day.

The Eucharist plays a central role in Christian life. First, it affects the way people relate to one another. Secondly, through the Eucharist, both forgiveness and a call to forgive is experienced. Thirdly, the Eucharist nourishes a community through the Word and Life of Christ.[18]

It is the daily viaticum and source of the spiritual life for the individual and for the community. By means of the Eucharist, all catechists or youth ministers are called to live Christ's Paschal Mystery, uniting themselves to him by offering their own lives to the Father through the Holy Spirit. Frequent and prolonged adoration of Christ present in the Eucharist enables us in some way to relive Peter's experience at the Transfiguration: "It is well that we are here."[19] In the celebration of the mystery of the Lord's Body and Blood, the unity and charity of those who have dedicated their lives to God are strengthened and increased.

It is our intimacy with the Lord in the Holy Eucharist that, at one and the same time, makes us conscious of our own sinfulness and inflames our desire to live always in Christ and, therefore, to love as He loves.[20]

As catechists or youth ministers we must be fervent witnesses to Christ's presence on the altar. Let the Eucharist mould our life and the life of the people we will form. Let it guide all life's choices. The Eucharist, the true and living presence of the love of the Trinity, inspire in us ideals of solidarity and lead us to live in communion with our brothers and sisters in every part of the world.

Conclusion

Seeing the Eucharist as a whole, a person will appreciate and value its true meaning and effect on one's life. The Eucharist as the memorial of Christ's Passover makes it presents to the memory of the believers the sacramental offering which is his Body that they may conform their lives to Christ (*Memorial*). It is a mystery that surpasses our understanding and can only be received in faith. Thus, when we receive him with faith we will be able to surrender ourselves in contemplation *(Mystery of Faith)*. As Christ is present in the Eucharist, in the sacrament of his death and resurrection,*(Paschal Mystery)*so it is, in the anticipation of the heavenly glory and every time this mystery is celebrated *(Eschatological summit)*. Indeed, it is the cause of communion in the divine life and the unity of the People of God finding its source in love as it recalls makes presents and brings about charity *(Grace and Summit of the Life of the Ecclesial Community)*. Thanks to the Eucharist, it brings unity among believers as Chris continues to build his Church: he brings us together in praise and thanksgiving for salvation, in the communion which only infinite love can forge. Therefore, our gathering takes on its fullest meaning through the celebration of the Eucharist.

[1] "Blessed are those who have not seen and have believed."

[2]Cf. CCC 613

[3] Lk 22:19

[4] CCC 1362

[5] CCC 1363

[6] CCC 1364

[7]Cf. John Paul II and the Mystery of the Eucharist, p. 24

[8]Cf. Ecclesia de Eucharistia, 15

[9] Lk 22:19-20

[10] Mt 26:28

[11] CCC 1402

[12]Jn 6:54

[13] Cf. CCC 1405

[14] CCC 1324

[15] CCC 1325

[16] CCC 1396

[17]Cf. John Paul II and the Mystery of the Eucharist, p. 256

[18] https://www.romereports.com/en/2014/02/12/pope-s-audience-three-practical-ways-in-which-the-eucharist-can-improve-daily-life/

[19] Mt 17:4

[20]   http://www.catholicherald.co.uk/news/2012/08/16/how-the-eucharist-can-change-your-life/

CHAPTER NINE

The Blessed Virgin Mary

Introduction

The chapter on the Blessed Virgin Mary is divided into three headings namely: **Mary as the Masterpiece of the Trinity, Mary as the Mother of the Incarnate Word and of the Church** and **Mary as the Sign of Hope for the Pilgrim Humanity.**

Definition of Terms:

a. **Predestination** – The act of the divine Will determining Mary's existence, ordaining her to the beatific vision and, as a means to that end, charging her with a specific mission.

b. **Dogma** – A divinely revealed truth, proclaimed as such by such infallible teaching authority of the Church, and hence binding on all the faithful without exception, now and forever.

Our Catechism teaches us that: "What the Catholic faith believes about Mary is based on what it believes about Christ, and what it teaches about Mary illumines in turn its faith in Christ.[1]"

This leads us to the fundamental Marian principle through which other truths on the Blessed Virgin Mary flows unto and that is the Divine Motherhood. Mary was the one chosen to become the Mother of God.

Mary, The Masterpiece of the Trinity

The Second Vatican Council document on the Church Lumen Gentium mentions that Mary "is endowed with the high office and dignity of the Mother of the Son of God, and therefore she is also the beloved daughter of the Father and the temple of the Holy Spirit[2]"

Mary is the beloved daughter of the Father for she is seen as fulfilling a function of responsible service for the realization if God's salvific plan. She is the Daughter of Zion who stands out the poor and humble of the Lord, such as confidently hope for and receive salvation from Him.

Mary is the Temple of the Holy Spirit for it emphasizes the sacred character of the Virgin now the permanent dwelling of the Spirit of God. Through the Paraclete flowed forth the fullness of grace and the abundant grace to Her.

Everything comes from the will of the Father that is why Mary's predestination to be the Mother of God was purely gratuitous. She merited the Divine Motherhood in the order of execution out of fittingness. It means that God had bestow this prerogative on Mary, He endowed her with such degree of sanctity that she was worthy to become the Mother of God through the work of the Holy Spirit. Her degree of sanctity starts from the first moment of her conception (by her mother St. Anne), by a singular grace and privilege of almighty God and by virtue of the merits of Jesus Christ, Savior of the human race, that she was preserved immune from all stain of original sin[3]. This is what the Dogma of the Immaculate Conception teaches. Just as a woman had a share in the coming of death, so also should a woman contribute to the coming of life that is why Mary is called as the New Eve for she brought forth life and that life is the New Adam, Jesus Christ.

The Sacred Scriptures of the Old and the New Testament, show the role of the Mother of the Savior in the economy of salvation.

The books of the Old Testament describe the history of salvation by which the coming of Christ into the world was slowly prepared. Mary was already prophetically foreshadowed in:

- Genesis 3:15 – The Protoevangelium – The first good news that a promise of victory over the serpent which was given to our first parents after their fall into sin.

- Isaiah 7:14 and Micah 5: 2-3 – A Virgin shall conceive and bear a son, whose name will be called Emmanuel.

Mary, Mother of the Incarnate Word and Mother of the Church

After a long expectation of the promise, the fullness of time had came that God send forth His Son into the world and this was enfolded through the Annunciation[4], the time of fulfilment of God's promise.

In sending forth His Son, He wanted to prepare a body for His Son through the free cooperation of a creature. God chose a young Jewish woman of Nazareth in Galilee, "a virgin betrothed to a man whose name was Joseph, of the house of David; and the virgin's name was Mary."

The angel Gabriel salutes her as "full of grace". In fact, in order for Mary to be able to give the free assent of her faith to the announcement of her vocation, it was necessary that she be wholly borne by God's grace. It was mentioned that she would give birth to "the Son of the Most High" without knowing man, by the power of the Holy Spirit, Mary responded with the obedience of faith, certain that "with God nothing will be impossible": "Behold, I am the handmaid of the Lord; let it be done to me according to your word." Thus, giving her consent to God's word, Mary becomes the mother of Jesus.

Mary is acclaimed by Elizabeth, at the prompting of the Spirit and even before the birth of her son, as "the mother of my Lord".Hence the Church confesses that Mary is truly "Mother of God" (*Theotokos*)[5]. The Church has confessed that Jesus was conceived solely by the power of the Holy Spirit in the womb of the Virgin Mary, affirming that He was conceived "by the Holy Spirit without human seed"[6] This is then Dogma of the Divine Motherhood of Mary.

In the virginal motherhood led the Church to confess Mary's real and perpetual virginity even in the act of giving birth to the Son of God made man. In fact, Christ's birth "did not diminish his mother's virginal integrity but sanctified it." And so the liturgy of the Church celebrates Mary as *Aeiparthenos*, the "Ever-virgin"[7]. This is then Dogma of the Perpetual Virginity of Mary.

Against the doctrine the objection is sometimes raised that the Bible mentions brothers and sisters of Jesus. The Church has always understood these passages as not referring to other children of the Virgin Mary. In fact James and Joseph, "brothers of Jesus", are the sons of another Mary, a disciple of Christ, whom St. Matthew significantly calls "the other Mary". They are close relations of Jesus, according to an Old Testament expression[8].

In the public life of Jesus, Mary makes significant appearances. At the wedding feast of Cana[9], moved with pity, she brought about by her intercession the beginning of miracles of Jesus the Messiah. In the course of her Son's preaching she received the words whereby in extolling a kingdom beyond the calculations and bonds of flesh and blood, He declared blessed those who heard and kept the word of God, as she was faithfully doing[10]. After this manner the Blessed Virgin advanced in her pilgrimage of faith, and faithfully persevered in her union with her Son unto the cross, where she stood, in keeping with the divine plan, she was given by her Son Jesus dying on the cross to His disciple, John as a mother with these words: "Woman, behold thy son."[11] Jesus proclaims the motherhood of Mary not only in relation to the Apostle John but also to every disciple.

The Blessed Virgin is also intimately united with the Church. While in the most holy Virgin the Church has already reached that perfection whereby she is without spot or wrinkle, the followers of Christ still strive to increase in holiness by conquering sin. And so they turn their eyes to Mary who shines forth to the whole community of the elect as the model of virtues.

Mary, Sign and Hope for the Pilgrim Humanity

Just as the Mother of Jesus, glorified in body and soul in heaven, is the image and beginning of the Church as it is to be perfected is the world to come, so too does she shine forth on earth, until the day of the Lord shall come, as a sign of sure hope and solace to the people of God during its sojourn on earth.[12] In brief, this is the Dogma of Mary's Assumption into Heaven.

In Mary, we contemplate what the Church already is in her mystery on her own "pilgrimage of faith," and what she will be in the homeland at the end of her journey. There, "in the glory of the Most Holy and Undivided Trinity," "in the communion of all the saints, " the Church is awaited by the one she venerates as Mother of her Lord and as her own mother[13].

In the meantime, the Mother of Jesus, in the glory which she possesses in body and soul in heaven, is the image and beginning of the Church as it is to be perfected in the world to come. Even when she was taken up to heaven her constant intercession continued to bring us the gifts of eternal salvation. By her maternal charity, she cares for the brethren of her Son, who still journey on earth surrounded by dangers and cults, until they are led into the happiness of their true home.

Pastoral Application

We must keep in mind the centrality and primacy of Christ in everything – the Blessed Virgin Mary, the saints, the sacraments, word of life, devotions, etc. – must be taught in relation to Christ, and with the purpose of leading the catechized into intimacy with Christ[14].

We Catholics do not worship or adore Mary. In the scheme of worship and veneration, we must be reminded that the worship given to God alone is called *Latria*, the highest type of religious reverence. While the reverence we pay to the saints and angels is called *Dulia*. And the reverence we offer to Mary, the Mother of God is called *Hyperdulia* which is higher than that offered to the other saints and to the angels.

We should venerate Mary out of love for her and appreciation of her dignity, not primarily to obtain personal or material favours [15]. We the Filipinos are called Pueblo Amante de Maria – A People in Love with Mary[16]

To conclude, the things that we have said earlier, in summary, are part of the Church's Dogma on the Blessed Virgin Mary which are: The Divine Motherhood, Perpetual Virginity, Immaculate Conception and Assumption into Heaven.

[1] CCC 487
  [2] LG 53
  [3] Ineffabilis Deus
  [4] Luke 1: 26-38
  [5] CCC 495
  [6] CCC 496
  [7] CCC 499
  [8] CCC 500
  [9] John 2: 1-12
  [10] Mark 6: 1-6a
  [11] LG 58
  [12] LG 68
  [13] CCC 972
  [14] PCP II no. 157
  [15] AMB 81
  [16] PCP II, no. 153

CHAPTER TEN

The Christian Life

INTRODUCTION:

Christian Life as life in Christ directed to God: faith-hope-charity as the grace of connaturality and as a personal response in communion with God and with others.

Definition of Terms

- <u>GRACE</u> is the gratuitous gift that God gives us to make us of his own life, infused by the Holy Spirit into man's soul to heal its sin and sanctify it. It is a GRATUITOUS GIFT, which depends entirely on God's gratuitous initiative and surpasses the abilities of the intellect and the powers of human beings.[1]

- <u>VIRTUES</u> are acquired by education, by deliberate acts and by a perseverance ever-renewed in repeated efforts are purified and elevated by divine grace. With God's help, they forge character and give facility in the practice of the good. The virtuous man is happy to practice them.[2]

*To distinguish grace from virtues: **We ask for GRACE necessary to persevere in the pursuit of the VIRTUES in order to maintain our moral balance.[3]***

- <u>THEOLOGICAL VIRTUES</u> are faith, hope and charity. Human virtues are rooted in the theological virtues which adapt man's faculties for participation in the divine nature. These are virtues that relate directly to the Triune God.[4]

- St. Thomas Aquinas speaks of <u>CONNATURALITY</u> where things or beings can be connatural to each other in the sense that they have the same nature. Something can be connatural to a being insofar as it *becomes natural through habituation*, because "custom is a second nature."[5]

THEOLOGICAL POINT OF VIEW

<u>Can man live a Christian life directed to God despite his sinfulness?</u>

Genesis 1:27, says, *"God created man in his image; in the divine image he created him; male and female he created them."* But because of disobedience, death makes an entrance into human history.[6] The personal sin of Adam & Eve affected human nature which is transmitted to all mankind. The transmission of original sin deprives human nature of holiness and justice.[7] Man's nature is wounded in the natural powers proper to it, subject to ignorance, sufferings, and the dominion of death, and inclined to sin. The consequences for nature, weakened and inclined to evil, persist in man and summons him to spiritual battle.

But human nature has not been totally corrupted. Through **baptism**, original sin is erased and the man goes back toward God. In baptism, man receives **filial adoption**, where he becomes the child of God and takes on God's divine nature, a member of Christ and co-heir with him, and a temple of the Holy Spirit.[8] This will then give him the ability to follow Christ. It makes him capable of acting rightly and doing good. The baptized are given sanctifying grace, enabling them to believe in God, hope in him and love him through the *theological virtues;* giving them the power to live and act under the prompting of the Holy Spirit through its gifts; allowing them to grow in goodness through the *moral virtues.* In union with his Savior, the disciple attains the perfection of charity which is holiness. Being matured in grace, the moral life blossoms into eternal life in the glory of heaven.[9]

The disfigured image of God in man is restored to its original beauty as a divine image and ennobled by the grace of God.[10] It takes on the image of Christ the Redeemer and who is the image of the invisible God. Therefore, divine image is present in every man.

Are baptism and its effects enough for us to live a Christian life?

Man does not just rely on receiving baptism and its effects to live a Christian life directed to God. He has to conform to the life of Jesus as an OBEDIENT SON OF THE FATHER and IMAGE OF GOD'S MERCY AND COMPASSION TO OTHERS. He is "the perfect man,"[11] who invites us to become his disciples and follow him. In humbling himself, he has given us an example to imitate, through his prayer, he draws us to pray, and by his poverty, he calls us to accept freely the privation and persecutions that may come our way.[12]

Whoever is called "to teach Christ" must first seek "the surpassing worth of knowing Christ Jesus"; he must suffer "the loss of all things. . ." in order to "gain Christ and be found in him", and "to know him and the power of his resurrection, and (to) share his sufferings, becoming like him in his death, that if possible (he) may attain the resurrection from the dead"[13]

How does man conform to the life of Christ? Is it possible, given man's sinfulness and Jesus is the perfect man and God?

It is not easy for man, wounded by sin, to maintain moral balance. Christ's gift of salvation offers us the grace necessary to persevere in the pursuit of the virtues. Everyone should always ask for this grace of light and strength, frequent the sacraments, cooperate with the Holy Spirit, and follow his call to love what is good and shun evil.[14]

Theological virtues: faith-hope-love is the foundation of Christian moral activity; they animate it and give it its special character. They inform and give life to all the moral virtues. The **Holy Spirit plays an important role** in giving the faithful the grace to be able to conform to the life of Christ. [15]**Therefore, the virtues of faith, hope and love as the grace of connaturality make it possible for a man to live a Christian life.**

FAITH is the theological virtue by which we believe in God and all that he has revealed to us and that the Church proposes for our belief because God is Truth itself. By faith, the human person freely commits himself to God. Therefore, the believer seeks to know and do the will of God because "faith works through charity."[16]

HOPE is a theological virtue by which we desire and await from God eternal life as our happiness, placing our Christ's promise trust in and relying on the help of the grace of the Holy Spirit to merit and to persevere to the end of our earthly life[17]

CHARITY is the theological virtue by which we love God above all things and our neighbour as ourselves for the love of God. Jesus makes charity the new commandment, the fullness of the law. "It is the bond of perfection" (Colossians 3:14) and the foundation of the other virtues to which it gives life, inspiration, and order. Without charity "I am nothing" and "I gain nothing" (1 Cor 13:1-3).[18]

As man partakes in the life of Jesus, he also partakes in His PASCHAL MYSTERY, which is His passion, death and resurrection. In Mark 8:34, Jesus said, *"Whoever wishes to come after me must deny himself, take up his cross, and follow me."* Jesus forewarned the disciples of the suffering they will bear. Parallel with Luke 9:23 it says, *"If anyone wishes to come after me, he must deny himself and take up his cross daily and follow me."* The word **"daily"** was added in this version, which can be interpreted as a shriller warning of difficulties and hardships.

In order for man to resurrect from each and every death, he needs to habituate with the theological virtues until it becomes his second nature, by the grace of connaturality. As man becomes faithful, hopeful and charitable, he is sustained to be constantly in communion with God and communion with others.

With faith, hope and love, how then can man respond to being constantly in Communion with God and neighbour?

The virtues of FAITH, HOPE and LOVE become the main ingredients of COMMUNION which becomes the fruit of obedience of man to Jesus' greatest commandment as it says in Luke 10:27, *"You shall love the Lord, your God, with all your heart, with all your being, with all your strength and with all your mind and your neighbour as yourself."* The concept of communion always involves a double dimension: the vertical (communion with God) and the horizontal (communion among men). It is essential to the Christian understanding of communion that it be recognized above all as a gift from God and as a fruit of God's initiative carried out in the paschal mystery. The new relationship between man and God, that has been established in Christ and is communicated through the sacraments, also extends to a new relationship among human beings.[19] Saint Paul said in 1 Corinthians 13:13, *"So faith, hope, love remain, these three; but the greatest of this is love."* To love therefore is an act that directs Christians to the life of Christ through the Holy Spirit.

PASTORAL APPLICATION

We are all called to live a Christian life. A life conformed to Christ who was an obedient Son of God and who redeemed all of us from our sin through His passion, death and resurrection. Conforming to His life is to obey God's commandments which is to love Him and to love others. Furthermore, Jesus has shown how to live an obedient life to the Father through His words and deeds. He has taught us how to pray and live a faithful and moral life through the "Lord's Prayer,"[20] "Beatitudes"[21] and all other teachings in the Gospel. The public ministry of Jesus is a perfect model for us to mature in our Christian life. We follow Him when He said in Matthew 28:19-20, *"Go, therefore, and make disciples of all nations, baptizing them in the name of the Father, and of the Son, and of the Holy Spirit, teaching them to observe all that I have commanded you. And behold, I am with you."*

Jesus promised His disciples of being with them always by sending another Advocate. [22] We too can hang on to that promise and rely on the Holy Spirit for that call to discipleship.

Being a Christian is more than just being baptized. Practices like prayers, devotions, sacraments, and bible studies are all good. But to be a Christian goes even beyond those practices. It even goes beyond what we say or what we post on our social media accounts. Saint Francis of Assisi said, *"Preach the Gospel every day, if necessary use words."* It takes more than words to become a true

Christian and a true disciple of God.

I may not be a preacher, a teacher or a full-time mission worker to be able to preach God's words. But through loving thoughts, words and actions, I can be a disciple and bring Christ to others in my daily life at work, in the parish community, with family and friends. I may even go beyond my circle, by helping the poor, the sick and the needy and caring for the environment that they live in.

The Christian life is a life focused on God. The God who initiated love on us despite our sinfulness. We were redeemed by Jesus, out of love. The love which is given by the Holy Spirit, through which we are able to be in communion with God and with others.

[1] CCC 1999

[2] CCC 1820

[3] CCC 1811

[4] CCC 1812

[5] The Natural, The Connatural, and The Unnatural by J. Budziszewski

[6] CCC 400

[7] CCC 404

[8] CCC 1265

[9] CCC 1709

[10] CCC 1701

[11] GS 38

[12] John 13:15

[13] CCC 428

[14] CCC 1811

[15] CCC 1813

[16] Compendium of the Catechism of the Catholic Church 386 (CCC#1814-1816, 1842)

[17] Compendium of the Catechism of the Catholic Church 387 (CCC#1817-1821, 1843)

[18] Compendium of the Catechism of the Catholic Church 388 (CCC#1822-1829, 1844)

[19] CONGREGATION FOR THE DOCTRINE OF THE FAITH LETTER TO THE BISHOPS OF THE CATHOLIC CHURCH (IN SOME ASPECTS OF THE CHURCH UNDERSTOOD AS COMMUNION 3)
[20] Matthew 6:9-13 (CCC 2761)
[21] Mathew 5:3-12 (CCC 1716)
[22] John 15:16

CHAPTER ELEVEN

Christian Action

THE FUNDAMENTAL PRINCIPLES OF CHRISTIAN ACTION (WORK): "to imitate the Father" (Mt. 5:48; Lk. 6:36), "to live in Christ" (Rom. 8:1), "to walk in the spirit" (Gal. 5:25)

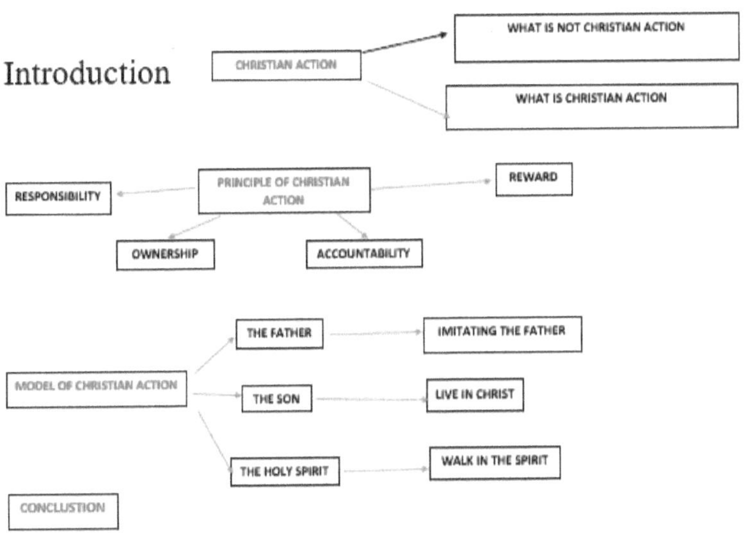

CHRISTIAN ACTION

WHAT IS NOT CHRISTIAN ACTION

Christian action is not just Human activity motivated by friendship, neighbourliness, and brotherhood. It is not just the performance of Church duties or religious "busyness" or anything we 'do'.

Many of us think that Christian action is Normal, civilized good behaviour. It is limited to times when one is "moved by the spirit". It is a service in church organizations. But basically, these are our misconceptions about Christian action.

WHAT IS CHRISTIAN ACTION

Christian action is both an expression and a consequence of our love of God. It is a realization that we are called to love our neighbour because we are loved by God. Our actions become Christian when our motivations are elevated and empowered by God's love and grace for the spreading of the kingdom of God.

In fact, authentic Christian Action springs from love for God and love for neighbour. Our personal commitment to Christ reflects a fundamental change in the direction of our lives and in all our relationships with others. Christian love is more than affection, more than giving time, energy or things. Christian love is having the attitude of Christ for another person, showing respect, genuine concern, and steadfast commitment. The total giving of oneself for another for the love of God is the measure of a person's human and spiritual development.

Christian action is a way of bringing God's love to the world. Our task as Christians is to discover God's will for our lives so that our lives will make real God's love for the world. Christian action flows from our own encounters with Christ and our encounters with God's children. Christian action is often where our pain and brokenness meet the world's pain and brokenness. Christian action is consistent with our personal gifts and abilities. Christian action is informed by the special concern we are to have for the poor and lonely and lost. Christian action empowers others. Christian action empowers us. It often rewards us with more than we have given.

PRINCIPLE OF CHRISTIAN ACTION

OWNERSHIP

At the beginning of Genesis, God creates everything and puts Adam in the Garden to work and take care of it. It is clear that man was created to work and that *work is the stewardship of all of the creation that God has given him.* This is the fundamental principle of biblical stewardship. God owns everything, we are simply managers or administrators acting on his behalf. Therefore, stewardship expresses our obedience regarding the administration of everything God has placed under our control, which is all-encompassing. Stewardship is the commitment of one's self and possessions to God's service, recognizing that we do not have the right of control over our property or ourselves.

RESPONSIBILITY

While God has graciously entrusted us with the care, development, and enjoyment of everything he owns as his stewards. We are called as God's stewards to manage that which belongs to God, we are responsible to manage his holdings well and according to his desires and purposes.

ACCOUNTABILITY

A steward is one who manages the possessions of another. We are all stewards of the resources, abilities and opportunities that God has entrusted to our care, and one day each one of us will be called to give an account for how we have managed what the Master has given us. God has entrusted authority over the creation to us and we are not allowed to rule over it as we see fit. We are called to exercise our dominion under the watchful eye of the Creator managing his creation in accord with the principles he has established.

Like the servants in the Parable of the Talents, we will be called to give an account of how we have administered everything we have been given, including our time, money, abilities, information, wisdom, relationships, and authority. We will all give account to the rightful owner as to how well we managed the things he has entrusted to us.

REWARD

In <u>Colossians 3:23-24</u> Paul writes:

Whatever you do, work at it with all your heart, as working for the Lord, not for men, since you know that you will receive an inheritance from the Lord as a reward. It is the Lord Christ you are serving.

The Bible shows us in the parables of the Kingdom that faithful stewards who do the master's will with the master's resources can expect to be rewarded incompletely in this life, but fully in the next.

We all should long to hear the master say what he exclaims in Matthew 25:21: *Well done, good and faithful servant! You have been faithful with a few things; I will put you in charge of many things. Come and share your master's happiness!*

As Christians in the 21st century, we need to embrace this larger biblical view of stewardship, which goes beyond church budgets or building projects, though important; it connects everything we do with what God is doing in the world.

We need to be faithful stewards of all God has given us within the opportunities presented through his providence to glorify him, serve the common good and further his Kingdom.

MODEL

THE FATHER

To imitate the Father (Mt. 5:48: *Do not even the gentiles do as much? You must therefore be perfect, just as your heavenly Father is perfect.* **Luke 6:36:** *Be compassionate just as your Father is compassionate***)**

God calls each of us to be loving, kind, gentle, holy, God calls us to be people who live out our daily lives with integrity. God is with us every moment of every day. When we are driving our car, we can have a conversation with Him. When we are washing dishes, we can sing praise to Him. When we face a big decision in our life, we can ask our Heavenly Father to lead and guide us. God cares about the detail of our life, He wants to be in an intimate, loving, deep relationship with us.

THE SON JESUS CHRIST

To live in Christ (Rom 8:1 *Thus, condemnation will never come to those who are in Christ Jesus***)**

The phrase 'in Christ Jesus' refers to us being joined to and united with Christ, the second Adam. It simply means 'under the control of', under the influence of, in close association with.

Therefore, if we are "in Christ Jesus" we have this Spirit of life working in us. And every Christian is "in Christ Jesus." That's what being a Christian means: being united to Christ by faith in all that God is for us in Jesus.

The importance of the phrase "to live in Christ" cannot be overstated. In all honesty, this phrase should be central to every Christian's life. In this statement, the apostle Paul is saying that everything he has tried to be, everything he is, and everything he looked forward to being pointed to Christ. From the time of Paul's conversion until his martyrdom, every move he made was aimed at advancing the knowledge, gospel, and church of Christ. Paul's singular aim was to bring glory to Jesus.

"To live in Christ" means that we proclaim the gospel of Christ. Paul preached in synagogues; he preached at riversides; he preached as a prisoner; he preached as an apostle; he preached as a tentmaker. He brought the message of Christ's sacrifice to kings, soldiers, statesmen, priests, and philosophers, Jews and Gentiles, men and women. He would preach to literally anyone who would listen.

"To live in Christ" means that we imitate the example of Christ. Everything that Jesus did and said, that's what Paul wanted to do and say. "To live in Christ" means that we pursue the knowledge of Christ. We want to know Christ better and better each day. Not just a set of facts about Christ, but Christ Himself. "To live in Christ" means that we are willing to give up anything that prevents us from having Christ. We cling to the promise of our Lord in (Mark 10:29-30) that our sacrifices for Jesus' sake will be repaid a hundredfold. "To live in Christ" means that Christ is our focus, our goal, and our chief desire. Christ is the center point of our mind, heart, body and soul. Everything that we do, we do for Christ's glory. As we run the "race marked out for us," we lay aside the entangling sin and worldly distractions, "fixing our eyes on Jesus" (Hebrews 12:1-2). He is our life.

THE HOLY SPIRIT

To walk in the Spirit (Gal 5:25 *Since we are living by the Spirit, let our behaviour be guided by the Spirit***)**

"Walking in the Spirit is the active application of our faith in Jesus Christ to overcome in this world." If faith is the key to our life of transformation and victory through Jesus Christ in the New Covenant, then Walking in the Spirit is the active application of our faith to achieve those ends. It is the work of the Spirit to change us into the likeness of Christ (2 Corinthians 3:17-18) and it is through Walking in the Spirit that this is achieved in us.

We are at war! When we walk in the Spirit we are able to fight and defeat the evil that comes against us. We should not mistake, when we are Christian we are at war, but not war as this world understands it. The war we are waging is against the evil spiritual realm and is not of this world (2 Corinthians 10:3-6). So too then the weapons of our warfare also are not of this world but are of divine power.

What is walking in the Spirit?

"But I say walk by the Spirit and you do not gratify the desires of the flesh" Galatians 5:16 "For all who are led by the Spirit of God are sons of God" Romans 8:14 "He condemned sin in the flesh in order that the just requirement of the law would be fulfilled in us who walk not according to the flesh, but according to the Spirit." Romans 8:3-4?

Galatians 5:16-26 shows that if you walk by the Spirit you do not gratify the desires of the flesh which are opposed to the desires of the Spirit, and those who belong to Christ Jesus have put to death the passions and desires of the flesh. In order to please God, you must worship Him in Spirit and truth because God is Spirit (John 4:23-24). This again is emphasised by Paul in Romans 8:3-9 who shows that the just requirement of the law is fulfilled in those who walk according to the Spirit. He further shows that to set your mind on the flesh is death, but to set your mind on the Spirit is life and peace, and that the mind set on the flesh cannot please God because it is hostile to God's way. So you see, there is a recurring theme in all of these passages. All of them indicate that a change must take place within you, led by the Spirit, and that change is in the way you think. It is your thoughts, driven by your desires that bring forth sin and death (James 1:14-15). It is because of this that the writer of Hebrews says that sin "...clings so closely..." and that you must lay it aside if you are to move forward in Christ (Hebrews 12:1).

How do you walk in the Spirit?

You are called to, "...take every thought captive to obey Christ..." as mentioned above, but how do you do this? In Philippians 4:8-9 Paul shows you that you should think and set your minds upon whatever is true, honourable, just, pure, lovely, gracious, excellent or worthy of praise. Thinking about these things is the application of Walking in the Spirit. So when you are being tempted, suffering or your desires and emotions are running amok... change your thinking by setting your mind on one of these things, and the "God of peace will be with you".

An Example of Walking in the Spirit: In Acts 16:19-40 we see Paul and Silas having been beaten and thrown into prison. While they would have been forgiven for grumbling at their misfortune, they did not complain but rather exercised their faith through Walking in the Spirit by prayer and singing hymns to God. What is more, the prisoners listened to them. At around midnight, an earthquake shook the foundations of the prison, the doors were opened and every one's fetters were unfastened. As a result, the jailer was about to kill himself, believing the prisoners had escaped, when Paul and Silas called out to him. Instead, the jailer found God with his family, Paul and Silas were fed and had their wounds cleaned and the following day left the town with an apology from the leaders of the city.

Finally, there are the promises from God that He will not allow you to be tempted beyond your strength but with the temptation will provide you with the way of escape that you may endure it (1 Corinthians 10:13). The way of escape is through Walking in the Spirit as it is by this process you hand the temptation or the problem over to Him to lead us through. And when you have come through and endured the trials, God himself will, "...restore, establish and strengthen you" (1 Peter 5:10).

Conclusion:

All of us are created by God, loved and saved in Jesus Christ, and fulfil ourselves by creating a network of multiple relationships of love, justice and solidarity with other persons while we go about our various activities in the world. Our action or work or activity, when it aims at promoting the integral dignity and vocation of the person, the quality of living conditions and the meeting in solidarity of peoples and nations, is in accordance with the plan of God. In short, when our actions or works are inclined toward the fulfilment of God's plan, it simply can be called Christian Action. As children of God, we all are invited to carry out Christian action as long as we are in this world.

CHAPTER TWELVE

Christian Living

INTRODUCTION:

Man is created by God and destined to end with God. He draws the purpose of life from this end will shape his conscious actions. Anything that reinforces man to this end would be described as good while anything that opposes it is evil. God always acts first and reveals himself to us. God created man in his own image and likeness. Man is redeemed by the BLOOD of CHRIST. Through HIM, we become CHILDREN OF GOD and partakers of the divine nature. We are made HOLY by the presence of the HOLY SPIRIT.

Therefore, we <u>respond</u> to GOD'S LOVE AND GRACE through our <u>actions</u> that would reflect the glory of God. The moral life, therefore, is a response "due to the many gratuitous initiatives taken by God out of love for man" (VS 10). Therefore, Christians are called to lead a life worthy of the gospel of Christ. (CCC1692)

"to imitate the Father" (c.f. Mt 5:48; Lk 6:36)

Jesus Christ always did what is pleasing to the Father, and always lived in perfect communion with Him. Likewise, as Christ's disciples, we are invited to live in the sight of the Father "who sees in secret: in order to become as your heavenly Father is perfect." (CCC 1693)

"to live Christ" (cf. Rom 8:1)

Incorporated into Christ by Baptism, Christians are "dead to sin and alive to God in Christ Jesus" and to participate in the life of the Risen Lord. Following Christ and united with Him, Christians can strive to be "imitators of God as beloved children, and walk-in love" by conforming their thoughts, words and actions to the "mind... which is yours in Christ Jesus," and by following his example. (CCC194)

"to walk in the Spirit" (cf.Gal.5:25)

"Justified in the name of the Lord Jesus Christ and in the Spirit of our God, "sanctified"...(and) called to be saints," Christians have become the temple of the Holy Spirit. This "SPIRIT of the SON" teaches them to ray to the Father and having become their life, prompts them to act so as to bear "THE FRUIT OF THE SPIRIT" by a charity in action. Healing the wounds of sin, the HOLY SPIRIT renews us interiorly through a spiritual transformation. He enlightens and strengthens us to live as "CHILDREN OF LIGHT' through all that is good, right and true. (CCC1695)

B. DEFINITION OF TERMS:

a. **Human Act** - it is an act done by humans that involve the exercise of judgement and will

b. **Human Freedom**- Condition in which human may freely choose their own behaviour and situations without external coercion or oppression

- Freedom is the power, rooted in reason and will, to act or not to act, to do this or that, and to perform deliberate actions on one's own responsibility. (CCC 1744)

c. **Conscience** - is a judgement of reason by which the human person recognizes the moral quality of a concrete act. (CCC 1796)

-Is man's most secret core, and his sanctuary. Therefore, he is alone with God whose voice echoes in his depths. (GS 16)

d. **Sin** - Theologically, sin is the human condition or qualities that are considered to be good according to moral religious standards.

e. **Virtue** - a disposition when habits or qualities that are considered to be good according to morals or religious standards.

Christian Living

We distinguish acts or deeds done by the agent(man) as **human acts** and acts of the **human person**. A human **act** is an act that involves the exercise of the judgement of the will. This act is done with full knowledge and of their own will, thus, man is responsible for his action. On the other hand, acts human person is instinctive reactions without the exercise of intellect and will. These actions are not concerned with morals since they are not voluntary.

The human **act** requires *human knowledge* and *human freedom*. In this case, we presume that if *human knowledge* is present, the person is aware of the rightness and the wrongness of what he is about to do. Human freedom for this matter is a condition in which humans freely choose their own behaviour and situation without external coercion or oppression. *Freedom* is the power rooted in reason and will to act or not to act, to do this or that, and to perform deliberated action on one's own responsibility. (CCC 1731) It refers to the internal or psychological freedom to decide and not the *internal freedom* to carry out one's decision.

We are free to choose what we are to do, but we are not free to make what we have chosen good or evil, right or wrong. Our choices are good or bad in so far they conform to God's divine and eternal laws, which are made known to us through the meditation of **conscience**. **Conscience** is the judgement of the intellect on the goodness or evil of an act performed or about to be performed. It is the "judgement of reason whereby the human person recognizes the moral quality of a concrete act that he is going to perform, is in the process of performing, or has already completed" (CCC 1778)

"Conscience is not an infallible judge" (VS 62). A right conscience is a judgment of a person who judges as good that which is truly good and judges as the evil which is truly evil. On the other hand, there is also erroneous conscience when people make a judgement of science that is mistaken.

Conscience must be informed and moral judgement enlightened. A well-formed conscience is upright and truthful. It formulates judgements according to reason, in conformity with the true good willed by the wisdom of the Creator. The education of conscience is indispensable for human beings who are subjected to negative influences and tempted by sin to prefer their own judgement and reject authoritative teachings. (CCC 1783)

In the Bible, sin is always understood as a refusal to do the will of God. What God wants is that we should love God and love one another, that we should be thoroughly moral people (CCC 1850). One example is the parable of the Prodigal Son in the gospel (Lk 15: 11-32). The Prodigal Son, having spent his time and money, returned home and asked for his Father's forgiveness. In sinning against his father, the Prodigal Son sinned against heaven. When we fail to love one another, by that very fact that we fail to love God, we damage our relationship with God, and we sin. The Bible also refers to a state or condition of sinfulness in which we find ourselves in the world.

Freedom has its goal the shaping of a moral character to be like Christ. The catechism describes the virtuous person as one who "tends towards the good with all his sensory and spiritual powers: he pursues the good and chooses it in concrete action" (CCC 1803). Virtue itself is described as " a habitual and firm disposition to do good." (CCC 1803)

PASTORAL APPLICATION

Formation of conscience should be given priority in Catechesis and Youth Ministry. According to PCP II, "it is evident that Christian discipleship or spirituality for social transformation demands a properly formed social conscience, the lack of it in many Filipinos is a major tragedy (PCP II 238). For conscience to develop properly, its moral tendency, discernment process and practical judgement must be rooted in Christ and the Holy Spirit, nourished by prayer and the Church's sacramental life and marked by an abiding fidelity to Christ and the Gospel through the Church magisterium. (PCP II 287)

CONCLUSION

The moral life is a response to God who first loved us. The response of humans depends on the gift of freedom and the awareness and the freedom to respond to God to shape our own lives in the image and likeness of God. The virtuous person uses freedom for virtuous acts. The responsible use of freedom is manifested particularly by a life of virtue. In doing so, we respond to God in love. When conscience is properly formed, it can bring a moral force to bear upon the social environment. Individuals would then be moved by their conscience to critique the social environment, reject and move against social structures, and set up in their stead those that allow and promote the flowering of a fuller life.

CHAPTER THIRTEEN

Diakonia

Introduction

The chapter on Diakonia is discussed based on the following: **Christ as "servant" of the Father, the Church as the servant of Christ, and the Christian as the servant of humankind.**

Definition of terms

Diakonia – This means "to serve", referring to the specific kind of help that we give to any people in need. Although the term *Diakonia* nowadays is associated with the Office of the Diaconate, part of the Holy Orders, thisgoes deeper than it seems as we dwell upon the *Diakonia* of Christ, and the Church, the People of God.

Christ, "servant" of the Father

"For the Son of Man did not come to be served but to serve and to give his life as a ransom for many."[1]

We believe that the Father, out of love for all of us, sent Christ so that we might have life through Him.[2] He lived among us, being like us in all things except sin[3]. Though being "in the form of God", "He emptied himself, taking the form of a slave, coming in human likeness; and found human in appearance, He humbled himself, becoming obedient to death, even death on a cross."[4] Being the "Servant" who carries out His Father's will in total obedience, Jesus became the instrument through which the will of the Father is accomplished, as what is said in the Gospel of Saint John: "And the Word became flesh and made His dwelling among us, and we saw His glory, the glory as of the Father's only Son, full of grace and truth."[5]

In the same way, He commissioned the Twelve to be His companions, sending them out to preach, and giving them the power to cast out demons[6]. As opposed to the lords and rulers who abuses their power, oppressing and exploiting others during their time, Jesus reminded them that a disciple must be ready to become a servant for all[7]. This was evident during the events of the last supper, where He washed the feet of the Apostles, giving them a model of what service they should give "so that as I have done for you, you should also do"[8]. Thus, the *Kyrios (Lord)* becomes the *Diakonos (Servant)*.

The Church, Servant of Christ

Christ founded the Church in order to continue His saving mission here on earth. She is endowed with the Gifts of her founder, receives the mission to proclaim and establish among all peoples the Kingdom of God[9], and because of that, being the people of God, we are called to serve just as Christ commanded to His Apostles: "You call me 'teacher' and 'master,' and rightly so, for indeed I am. If I, therefore, the master and teacher, have washed your feet, you ought to wash one another's feet."[10]

In the past, it is thought that "mission" is applied only to the clergy and religious who were sent to "foreign missions". But today, however, we must realize that "the obligation of spreading the faith is imposed on every disciple of Christ, according to his state."[11] In other words: all of us are called to mission. "All – without exception – are called to evangelize."[12]

Christian, servant of humankind

Our existence as Christians is a sharing in the *Diakonia* of Christ who fulfilled His mission in favor of mankind. Being a Christian means following the example of Christ not just through religious acts, but also in putting oneself at the service of others to the point of self-renunciation and self-giving, all for love, and this comes in form of the *ministries* that we do.

These ministries are not only limited to the liturgical services that we render, but also through different forms of fraternal charity, services to the physically and spiritually sick, to the needy, and to those who are imprisoned[13]. Therefore, the *Diakonia* is shown to be a fundamental determination of how should we live a Christian life, doing the mission which we have received in building up the Church and of our brothers and sisters in faith and love: "If anyone wishes to be first, he shall be the last of all and the servant of all."[14]

Pastoral Application

As Catechists and Youth Ministers, our participation in the life and mission of the Church is important for each of us has a gift from the Spirit to share, and each of us has also the need for the gift of others in building up the Church, the Body of Christ[15]. Saint John Paul II said: "Because of the one dignity flowing from Baptism, each member of the lay faithful, together with ordained ministers and men and women religious, shares a responsibility for the Church's mission."[16]

We must remember that *Diakonia* is a service among all various forms of services, whether it's within the Church's liturgical ministries or the good things we do for the people. It is a service in union with God through our Lord Jesus Christ, doing it in His name for "it is God who governs the world, not we. We offer Him our service only to the extent that we can, and for as long as he grants us the strength."[17]

Yet, despite the strength that we receive from Him, we also must remember that it is also a service born out of our weaknesses. It is powerful when it is powerless especially if we bear the sufferings and frailties of the poor and the oppressed. It is weak, for it suffers with the weaknesses of others, but strong with Christ. "Therefore, I am content with weaknesses, insults, hardships, persecutions, and constraints, for the sake of Christ; for when I am weak, then I am strong."[18]

Where there is the *diakonia*, there is God. His presence brings joy amidst sadness, healing in sickness, hope in despair, and love in hatred. It is the light shining from Him that prevails always over darkness.

[1] Mark 10:45

[2] 2^(nd) Plenary Council of the Philippines 37
[3] Cf. Hebrews 4:15
[4] Philippians 2:6-8
[5] John 1:14
[6] Mark 3:14-15
[7] Cf. Mark 10:42-43
[8] Cf. John 13:1-20
[9] Cf. Lumen Gentium 5
[10] John 13:13-14
[11] Lumen Gentium 17
[12] 2^(nd) Plenary Council of the Philippines 402
[13] Cf. Matthew 23:31-46
[14] Mark 9:35
[15] Cf. 1 Cor 12:4-36
[16] Christifideles Laici 15
[17] Deus Caritas Est 35
[18] 2 Cor 12:10

CHAPTER FOURTEEN

The Liturgy

INTRODUCTION

The Liturgy is the time of God and the space of God, and we must put ourselves there in the time and space of God and not look at the clock. The Liturgy is precisely to enter into the mystery of God; let yourself be led to the mystery and be in the mystery. In the celebration we enter the mystery of God, in that road that we cannot control he alone is the only one, he is the glory, he is the power. We ask for this grace, that the Lord teaches us to enter into the mystery of God.

In the New Testament, the word "liturgy" refers not only to the celebration of divine worship but also to the proclamation of the Gospel and to active charity. In all of these situations, it is a question of service of God and neighbour. In a liturgical celebration, the Church is a servant in the image of her Lord, the one "leitourgos"; she shares in Christ's priesthood (worship), which is both prophetic (proclamation) and kingly (service of charity) (CCC 1070)

Definition of Terms

<u>Liturgy</u> is the true worship of God, enacted by Jesus and his body (the Church), through the power of the Holy Spirit. It is a shared "public work" with ceremonies, rites, and formulas established by Scripture and Tradition. [you may also include the two movements in the liturgy - descending (sanctification) and ascending (glorification)

A ritual is defined as a religious or solemn ceremony consisting of a series of actions performed according to a prescribed order: e.g. ancient fertility rituals

Rite is a headline term that refers to a particular ceremony

---

http://www.vatican.va/news_services/liturgy/insegnamenti/ documents/ns_lit_doc_pieta-popolare-papa-francesco_it.html

THEOLOGICAL POINT OF VIEW

The Liturgy—Work of the Trinity: The Father—Source and Goal of the Liturgy

"Blessed be the God and Father of our Lord Jesus Christ, who has blessed us in Christ with every spiritual blessing in the heavenly places, even as he chose us in him before the foundation of the world, that we should be holy and blameless before him. He destined us before him in love to be his sons through Jesus Christ, according to the purpose of his will, to the praise of his glorious grace which he freely bestowed on us in the Beloved."[3] (CCC 1077)

Blessing is a divine and life-giving action, the source of which is the Father; his blessing is both word and gift.[4] When applied to man, the word "blessing" means adoration and surrender to his Creator in thanksgiving. (CCC 1078)

In the Church's liturgy, the divine blessing is fully revealed and communicated. The Father is acknowledged and adored as the source and the end of all the blessings of creation and salvation. In his Word who became incarnate, died, and rose for us, he fills us with his blessings. Through his Word, he pours into our hearts the Gift that contains all gifts, the Holy Spirit. (CCC 1082)

Christ's Work in the Liturgy

In the liturgy of the Church, it is principally his own Paschal mystery that Christ signifies and makes present. During his earthly life, Jesus announced his Paschal mystery by his teaching and anticipated it by his actions. The Paschal mystery of Christ, by contrast, cannot remain only in the past, because by his death he destroyed death, and all that Christ is - all that he did and suffered for all men - participates in the divine eternity, and so transcends all times while being made present in them all. The event of the Cross and Resurrection *abides* and draws everything toward life. (CCC 1085)

. . . is present in the earthly liturgy

"To accomplish so great a work" - the dispensation or communication of his work of salvation "*Christ is always present in his Church, especially in her liturgical celebrations.* He is present in the Sacrifice of the Mass not only in the person of his minister, 'the same now offering, through the ministry of priests, who formerly offered himself on the cross,' but especially in the Eucharistic species. (CCC 1088)

The Holy Spirit and the Church in the Liturgy

In the liturgy, the Holy Spirit is a teacher of the faith of the People of God and artisan of "God's masterpieces," the sacraments of the New Covenant. The desire and work of the Spirit in the heart of the Church is that we may live from the life of the risen Christ. When the Spirit encounters in us the response of faith which he has aroused in us, he brings about genuine cooperation. Through it, the liturgy becomes the common work of the Holy Spirit and the Church. (CCC 1091)

The Spirit and the Church cooperate to manifest Christ and his work of salvation in the liturgy. Primarily in the Eucharist, and by analogy in the other sacraments, the liturgy is the *memorial* of the mystery of salvation. The Holy Spirit is the Church's living memory.[19] (CCC 1099)

Christian liturgy not only recalls the events that saved us but actualizes them, and makes them present. The Paschal mystery of Christ is celebrated, not repeated. It is the celebrations that are repeated, and in each celebration, there is an outpouring of the Holy Spirit that makes the unique mystery present. (CCC 1104)

In the liturgy of the Church, God the Father is blessed and adored as the source of all the blessings of creation and salvation with which he has blessed us in his Son, in order to give us the Spirit of filial adoption. (CCC 1110)

Christ's work in the liturgy is sacramental: because his mystery of salvation is made present there by the power of his Holy Spirit; because his body, which is the Church, is like a sacrament (sign and instrument) in which the Holy Spirit dispenses the mystery of salvation; and because through her liturgical actions the pilgrim Church already participates, as by a foretaste, in the heavenly liturgy. (CCC 1111)

PASTORAL APPLICATION

The Church has liturgy in obedience to God. The sacramental rites of the New Testament fulfil and replace the Old Testament rituals. This is more clearly expressed by Christ's command at the Passover, *"Do this remembrance of me."* (Luke 22:19)

As true worship of God, it is also clear that the liturgy of the Church should follow the ceremonies, rites, and formulas established by the Scripture and Tradition where the will of God is revealed. As we are physical and social beings, it is fitting that the liturgy that God has given to us be public and engage our senses. Common prayers, visual signs, symbolic actions, sacred music, and the proclamation of the Scriptures are present in the Liturgy.

Liturgy, therefore, is a mystery to behold. It is in the liturgy where we can see, feel, hear, and even partake of the Body and Blood of Christ. We see the presence of God in three forms-- the consecrated Bread, in the person of the priest who represents Christ, and in the sacrifice of the Mass. We feel God's loving presence in the assembly gathered in the church. We hear God speak in the readings and in the Gospel. We are fed and nourished by the Eucharistic species.

The principle "Lex Orandi, Lex Credendi, Lex Vivendi" [translation: "the law of worship, so the law of belief, and so the law of life" or (better English) "As we Worship, so we believe, so we live."] It claims that <u>what we</u> pray or <u>celebrate liturgically</u> is what <u>we believe</u>; what we believe and celebrate (liturgically), <u>we live</u>. With this principle, we can argue how the liturgy (=RITUAL CELEBRATION) should and could spill into the LITURGY OF LIFE; and that both the ritual celebration and the liturgy of life are a

PROCLAMATION OF FAITH.

In the celebration of the Liturgy, it is God who never ceases to reach out to us. He invites us to know him, loves him, and serves him.